The
Scots-Irish
in the
Shenandoah Valley

by
BILLY KENNEDY

Causeway
PRESS

AMBASSADOR
PRODUCTIONS

First published July 1996

THE
SCOTS-IRISH CHRONICLES

Scots-Irish in the Hills of Tennessee

Scots-Irish in the Shenandoah Valley

~ *Coming Next* ~

Scots-Irish in Pennsylvania and the Carolinas

PRINTED IN NORTHERN IRELAND

Published by

Causeway Press
9, Ebrington Terrace,
Londonderry, BT47 1JS

Ambassador Productions Ltd,
Providence House
16, Hillview Avenue,
Belfast, BT5 6JR

Emerald House Group Inc.
1 Chick Springs Road, Suite 102
Greenville, South Carolina 29609

About *the Author*

BILLY KENNEDY is assistant editor of the Ulster/Belfast News Letter, Northern Ireland's leading morning newspaper and the oldest English language newspaper, having been founded in 1737. He was born in Belfast in 1943, but has spent almost his entire life living in Co. Armagh. He comes of Scots-Irish Presbyterian roots and has a deep fascination for his forebears of that tradition who moved to America in such large numbers during the 18th century. For the past 25 years, Billy Kennedy has been one of the leading journalists in Northern Ireland, covering the major stories of the Ulster troubles and as a prolific columnist on a variety of issues. He was a news editor with the News Letter for 18 years and in his present capacity as assistant editor of the newspaper, he is the leader writer and is also religious affairs, local government correspondent and literary editor. He is an authority on American country music and culture and has interviewed for the News Letter, Nashville personalities such as Garth Brooks, George Jones, Willie Nelson, Charley Pride, Ricky Skaggs, Kenny Rogers and Reba McEntire. For research on his books, 'The Scots-Irish in the Hills of Tennessee', published in 1995, and 'The Scots-Irish in the Shenandoah Valley', he travelled extensively through Virginia and Tennessee and met and talked with many Virginians and Tennesseans with direct links to the Scots-Irish settlers of 200 years ago. Billy Kennedy is also a specialist on sport and for 30 years he has written and compiled various publications for soccer internationally and on the local domestic football scene in Northern Ireland. He has been a director for 23 years of Linfield Football Club, Northern Ireland's leading soccer club. He has edited and compiled books on cultural traditions in Ireland, including two on the history of Orangeism in Ireland. He is married with a grown-up daughter.

Dedication

This book is dedicated to
my loving wife Sally, daughter Julie
and my parents.

Billy Kennedy

"Of making many books there is no END"
Ecclesiastes Chapter 12 Verse 12

~.~

The author acknowledges the help and support
given to him in the compilation of this book by
Samuel Lowry of Ambassador Productions;
Gregory Campbell of Causeway Press and Trey
Pennington, of Emerald House Group in the
United States.
Again it was wholeheartedly a team effort!

Cover: General Thomas Jonathan "Stonewall"
Jackson and General J.E.B. Stuart in the thick of
Civil War action. Paintings - Don Troini (Artist),
Southbury, Connecticut. Inset - President Woodrow
Wilson. Picture courtesy of Woodrow Wilson Birth-
place and Museum, Staunton, Virginia.

List of Contents

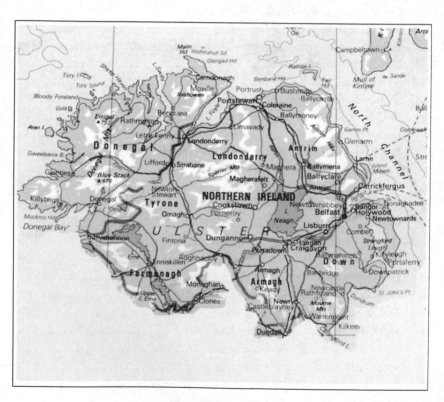

Northern Ireland

Foreword *from the United States*

Dr. John Rice Irwin

They call it the Shenandoah Valley of Virginia, and the liltingly beautiful sound of the name matches the immense beauty of the great valley itself. Its pristine character, fertile soil, plenteous water, and its abundant game did not long go unnoticed by those desirous of good land, a new home, and more freedom.

Many immigrants had moved from the "crowded" area on the east coast, especially from around Philadelphia, and into central Pennsylvania. Starting in the 1720s, the upper portion of the Shenandoah was settled, first in the vicinity around Staunton. This region's early history is tied closely with Scots-Irish, and the author points out that there was no place in America where the Scots-Irish settlers were more numerous and more influential.

Settlers soon came by the tens of thousands. When the migration continued, and much of the choice land was taken, the valley also served as a mighty passageway for those going into southwest Virginia, then into Tennessee, Kentucky, and on westward into Missouri, Kansas, and later into Texas and Oklahoma, and finally into the far west, especially into the northwest.

I don't know when Billy Kennedy first observed the romantic and historic aspects of the Shenandoah Valley, and the overwhelming influence his fellow Scots-Irish played in its settlement and development. I do know that he "had" to write about it, once he saw it. Billy approached the writing of this book "with a vengeance", as my grandfather would say. He "grabbed hold", read extensively, travelled to and fro, and talked with and interviewed countless local and regional historians, and he captured the flavour of the region, its history, and its people. Then he wrote. No dillydallying, no years, (or even weeks) of procrastinating. He wrote while the subject was fresh on his mind, and when the inspiration was strong.

Instead of dealing with the historical aspects of the valley in the more traditional sense, Billy has largely chosen to talk about the people themselves. Further, he tells of these people in a personal, human interest manner, while at the same time identifying with those qualities and accomplishments which brought them fame. The names of those with Scots-Irish ancestry connected with the Shenandoah is truly legion. Among this list are some of the most interesting, colorful, famous, and historically important figures in American history.

The book was written by a newspaperman, and by one who is a native of Northern Ireland. For these and other reasons, Billy Kennedy has provided us with a fresh look at one of our country's most interesting regions. It will, I think, enable us to understand, not only this small section of America, but it will do much to help us to understand the country as a whole, and it will help us to appreciate the contributions made by those noble folks known as the Scots-Irish. As Abraham Lincoln is reported to have said: "For those who like this type book, this is the type book they should read".

Dr. John Rice Irwin
Founder and Director, Museum of Appalachia,
Norris, Tennessee.

JOHN RICE IRWIN is founder and director of the Museum of Appalachia in Norris, Tennessee, a farm-village settlement which has gained publicity and acclaim throughout the United States. He is a former college, university and public school teacher and has served as both school principal and county school superintendent. He has also engaged successfully in farming, real estate, Appalachian Music (he has his own eight-member string band), and several small businesses and corporations which he started.

John Rice's main interest, however, lies in the people of his native Southern Appalachian Mountains. Since childhood he has spent virtually all his spare time visiting and talking with these mountain folk whom he admires and loves. He is considered to be one of the leading authorities on the history, culture, and people of Southern Appalachia, and on the American pioneer-frontier life in general.

John Rice Irwin is a prolific author, having written five books on life in the Southern Appalachian region:
• Musical Instruments of the Southern Appalachian Mountains - 1979.
• Guns and Gunmaking, Tools of Southern Appalachia - 1980.
• Baskets and Basket Making in Southern Appalachia - 1982.
• A People and Their Quilts - 1983.
• Alex Stewart, Portrait of a Pioneer - 1985.
These books are published by Schiffer Publishing, West Chester, Pennsylvania.

Born in 1930 of pioneer ancestors of a Scots-Irish and Welsh lineage, John Rice Irwin spent much of his childhood with his grandparents learning to love all aspects of Appalachian life and its colourful people. He joined the US Infantry during the Korean War and served two years. He has a degree in history and economics and a masters degree in international law.

John Rice Irwin has featured in dozens of national magazine articles (from Reader's Digest to Parade to Southern Living), thousands of newspaper stories, and featured in over a dozen nationally viewed TV documentaries.

He was chosen as "Citizen of the Year" in 1988 in his hometown of Norris and in 1989 was selected as one of 29 MacArthur Fellows in America, one of his country's most prestigious awards. He was the subject of a one-hour TV movie which was a year in the making, produced by the Parson's Foundation of Los Angeles.

He received the 1992 "Outstanding Marketing Professional" awarded presented by the Knoxville Chapter of the American Marketing Association and was awarded an honorary doctorate degree in Humane Letters from Cumberland College, Williamsburg, Kentucky in 1993 and an honorary doctorate of Humanities from Lincoln Memorial University, Harrogate, Tennessee in 1994.

Foreword *from Northern Ireland*

Councillor Dr. Ian Adamson, Lord Mayor of Belfast

B illy Kennedy continues his marvellous saga of the Ulster-Scots, which he began in his landmark study "The Scots-Irish in the Hills of Tennessee", by recounting the epic tale of the settlers of the Shenandoah Valley. During the reign of Queen Anne (1702-1714) the High Church Party in England had gained in strength and pressed for complete conformity in church practice.

In 1704, a Test Act was passed which required all officeholders in Ireland to take the sacrament of the Anglican Church. Presbyterians and other dissenters could not serve in the army, the militia, the civil service, the municipal corporations, the teaching profession or the Commission of the Peace. At Belfast the entire Corporation was expelled, and Londonderry lost ten of its twelve Aldermen (Schism Act). Coupled with this was English commercial avarice in restricting the Irish woollen trade, and the practice of rack renting by landlords, whereby a farmer's land could be sold to the highest bidder when his lease ran out. The final straw came with the drought of the 'Teen years of the 18th century. This ruined crops including flax, so that farmers, weavers and townspeople suffered alike. In 1716 sheep were afflicted with the "rot" and many died. Severe frosts ensued, prices soared and absentee English landlords steadily increased their rents. Thus began around 1717 the great migration of the Ulster people to America.

This migration was enough to arouse the English conscience, and in 1719 an Act of Parliament was passed to permit dissenters to celebrate their own form of worship. But rack renting continued, and from 1725 to 1729 there was such an exodus of Ulster Presbyterians to the southeastern tier of counties in Pennsylvania that their political influence quickly became considerable. This influence was directed increasingly against England. A "feedback" into Ulster itself helped to make it a centre of radicalism which was embodied in the establishment of the great newspaper the Belfast News Letter in 1737. The winter of 1739-1740 was known in Ulster as "the time of black frost" because of the darkness of the ice and the lack of sunshine. This severe weather caused famine all over the island, and a further wave of migration from Ulster from 1740-41. These new arrivals in America now generally went down through Pennsylvania into the Valley of Virginia and thus did the Ulstermen become the men of Shenandoah. Others crossed the first range of the Alleghenies to settle in the valleys of present Highland and Bath counties.

From Virginia the line of settlement passed into the Piedmount country of North and South Carolina and there, as in Virginia and Pennsylvania, German settlements were also effected. Countless German refugees - mostly Protestants - who had crowded into the Palatinate near Holland, had started migrating to Pennsylvania in the late 17th century. William Penn had invited them to live in his colony with the right to practice their faiths unmolested. In addition to Palatinates, Silesians, Alsatians and Moravians also came. The distinctive "Pennsylvanian Dutch" art, language and folkways of these German settlers still survives. Expert gunsmiths, the German settlers perfected the frontierman's long rifle, which the Scots-Irish were to use with such effect. Because of the close proximity of the two peoples the language of the Scots-Irish, Ulster-Scots or Scotch, which is a distinct language from English, influenced not only the English of Appalachia but also the low German of Pennsylvania-Dutch itself.

By the end of 1775 at least 250,000 Ulstermen and women had left Ireland over a period of 58 years, and, according to some estimates, formed one-sixth of the total population of the American colonies. To America they brought a hatred of that aristocratic landlordism exemplified by the Marquis of Donegall who had evicted many of the small farmers who could not pay the increased rents in his Co. Antrim estates. Lurgan (Co. Armagh)-born James Logan, the Provincial Secretary, had originally invited his fellow Ulstermen to Pennsylvania but soon complained that "a settlement of five families from the North of Ireland gives me more trouble than fifty of any other people". He found the Scots-Irish "troublesome settlers to the government and hard neighbours to the Indians".

Indeed, the first armed clash to precede the Revolutionary War occurred in 1771 when Scots-Irish settlers fought government forces on the Alamance River in North Carolina. On May 20, 1775 they were the most prominent signatories of the Mecklenberg Declaration of Independence drawn up in Charlotte, North Carolina. They subsequently supported the Declaration of Independence passed by the Continental Congress on July 4, 1776 and they composed the power and backbone of Washington's Army in the revolutionary war which followed. Their cause was advocated by the Belfast News Letter, the only major newspaper of the British Isles to publish in full the Declaration of Independence, and the contemporary Harcourt wrote that "the Presbyterians in the North are in their hearts, Americans". A German captain who fought alongside government forces was quite explicit: "call this war by whatever name you may, only call it not an American rebellion; it is nothing more or less than a Scots-Irish Presbyterian rebellion". The Pennsylvanian Line, the famous force of regular troops, was of primarily Ulster descent. The birthplace of New York State was the Ulster

County Court House, burned in 1777 by the British, who were aided by the Iroquois Indians under their hero, chieftain Joseph Brant.

The American Civil War of 1861-65 was to produce a galaxy of military leaders on both sides who had Ulster and Irish lineage. Ulysses Simpson Grant was commander-in-chief of the Union Army. When he became American President in 1868 he was said to preside over more Ulstermen than Queen Victoria. He was well served by General Philip Henry Sheridan, the cavalry commander who out-manoeuvred the Confederate commander-in-chief, Robert E. Lee and forced him to surrender at Appomatox on April 9, 1865. Later he became commander-in-chief of the American Army. General Lee was once asked: "What race makes the best soldiers?", to which the General replied, "The Scotch who came to this country by way of Ireland - because they have all the dash of the Irish in taking a position, and all the stubbornness of the Scotch in holding it".

My own favourite, and I suspect Billy Kennedy's as well, was the great Confederate General, Thomas Jonathan "Stonewall" Jackson, a simple God-fearing man who was outstanding and famed for his courage. His nom de guerre resulted from the heroic stand of his brigade at Bull Run on July 21, 1861. He defeated the Union forces at Ball's Bluff and in the Virginian campaign of 1862 he routed them and followed up by invading Maryland. His great-grandfather came from the Birches in Co. Armagh close to the shores of Lough Neagh. Only one man was victorious against Stonewall Jackson and he was General James Shields, an Ulster Roman Catholic, who was born in Altmore, Co. Tyrone, just 20 miles from the site of Stonewall Jackson's ancestral home. The Civil War pitted family against family, kinsman against kinsman, Scots-Irish against Scots-Irish.

W. F. Marshall has written: "On the Confederate side, North Carolina, home of the Ulster-Irish, led all the Southern states in enlisted men and then killed and wounded. In the North the pre-eminence goes to Pennsylvania, peopled in great measure by folk with the Ulster blood. The bloodiest single conflict of the war was fought between two regiments at Gettysburg, the 26th North Carolina Regiment and the 151st Pennsylvanian Regiment. Both regiments were practically wiped out. Well might Colonel Johnson say in 1889 'the greatest losses in the war occurred when the iron soldiers of North Carolina and Pennsylvania, descendants of the same race and stock, met on the field of battle, and locked arms in the embrace of death'."

James G. Leyburn's estimation of Scots-Irish influence in the formation of the early United States includes the following masterly assessment:

"Weber's idea of the Protestant ethic and Tawney's of the connection between Protestantism and the rise of capitalism do not find their most convincing example in the Scots-Irish; nevertheless, like other Calvinists, they believe in self-reliance, improving their own condition in life, thrift and hard work, the taking of calculated risks. They believed that God would prosper His elect if they, in turn, deserved this material reward by their conscientious efforts. Farmers, though they generally were, neither they nor their ancestors had been peasants in the sense of blind traditionalism of outlook. Their optimistic self-reliance, with a conviction that God helps those who help themselves, was to become the congenial American folk philosophy of the next century, not far removed from materialism and a faith in progress. The Scots-Irish were no more the originators of the ideas of freedom and individualism. What is significant is that, holding the attitude they did, and being present in such large numbers throughout most of the United States, they afforded the middle ground that could become typical of the American as he was to become. The Scots-Irish element could be the common denominator into which Americanism might be resolved". (1)

The people of Belfast and of all Ulster will be eternally grateful to Billy Kennedy for his continuing labours in bringing to a wider audience the history and achievements of the Scots-Irish in the United States of America. What can be more gratifying in this life than to hear a true soul sing of the deeds of his own people? What can be more satisfying on this earth than to read the story of the ordinary people, "oor ain folk" who created a new world out of a wilderness?

Dr. Ian Adamson
M.B., B.Ch., B.A.O. (Q.U.B.), D.C.H., R.C.P.S. (Glasgow)
D.C.H., R.C.S. (Dublin), M.F.C.H.
Lord Mayor of Belfast
June 3, 1996.

Footnote (1) James G. Leyburn, The Scotch-Irish : A Social History, Chapel Hill, The University of North Carolina Press, 1962.

The Scots-Irish *(Scotch-Irish) designation*

Scots-Irish is the term used to describe the people who settled in the American frontier in the 100 years from about 1717. Some in the United States today refer to the "Scotch-Irish", but this term now causes offence to many of the Scots-Irish tradition in Britain and America where "Scotch" is looked upon as an alcoholic spirit. In Northern Ireland the designation Ulster-Scot is very widely used by the Presbyterian descendants of the early frontier settlers. Nevertheless, for all the sensitivities it still touches upon, the term "Scotch-Irish" has an historical reality and utility. Ulsterman Francis Mackemie (Makemie), the founding father of the Presbyterian Church in America, was enrolled in the University of Glasgow in February, 1676 as "Franciscus Makemus Scoto-Hyburnus".

The form"Scotch-Irish" would have been used in the vernacular, as "Scotch" was the proper idiom until the 20th century for both language and people. "Scotch-Irish" had been used for the Ulster-Scots in America as early as 1695, but usually in a figurative way. The early Presbyterians from Ireland generally knew themselves simply as "Irish" and were thus known by the other colonists. The later establishment and rapid growth of highly visible Irish Roman Catholic communities led many Protestants in the United States to adopt the Scotch-Irish label.

★★★

Transatlantic partnership *from Ulster to Virginia*

Not all of the dreams and aspirations of the people of Ulster were brought to America in the 18th century. Some still continue into the 20th century in Northern Ireland and relate to the establishment in America of a museum that traces immigration to the New World and examine those various cultures that made the American nation what it is today.

In the 1970s a museum was opened in Omagh, Co. Tyrone, which exhibits life in Ulster in the 18th/19th century, demonstrating the reasons so many people were willing to leave their hard life behind in exchange for dreams and promises of a new world and a way of life. The Ulster American Folk Park, which this year celebrates its 20th anniversary, is a result of the efforts of Ulsterman Eric Montgomery, whose vision was responsible for that museum and the subsequent one in America.

Eric Montgomery, on visits to America, searched, but never found, a national museum that represented the humble pioneers who traced their ancestry back to ethnic roots in Europe, Africa and Asia. In the search of this dream Eric Montgomery discussed the creation of such a museum with the American International Bicentennial Committee, founded to plan international activities to celebrate America's 200th birthday. Although there was not sufficient time to create such a museum for that event, an international committee was formed to begin the process of examining the feasibility of organising such a museum. There were numerous states in America: Pennsylvania, the Carolinas, Kentucky,

Tennessee and Virginia which were all considered for the location of such a museum. It was Virginia that was selected. The selection came about as a result of two key factors: 1, the government of the Commonwealth of Virginia, authorised support for such a venture; 2, the site was to be located in the western part of the state alongside the routes taken by so many American immigrants who settled or passed through the "Great Wagon Road" opening up and creating America's frontier. This site, nestled in the Shenandoah Valley, was to become known as the "Gateway West".

This new American museum had its beginnings in 1986, ten years after the Ulster American Folk Park opened, and the strong ties established continued with its sister museum in Omagh during the early years. There have been exchanges of staff, artifacts, documentation, as well as even buildings thus developing a relationship that lives today as one of the most successful partnerships between museums anywhere in the world. The Museum of American Frontier Culture in itself is also a partnership between the Commonwealth of Virginia and a private foundation. It is a museum that commemorates the diverse ethnic backgrounds of many Americans and preserves the remarkable achievements of those people who came together from various countries to form a unique American way of life.

The Museum, located in Staunton, Virginia, brings to life for nearly 100,000 visitors a year, the trials and tribulations of the early settlers and the life they forged in an untamed wilderness. It also represents the shaping of America and how so many cultures and their people created a new nation. In America today, there are over 350 outdoor "living" museums, but nowhere is there one that has brought buildings from various countries into one setting in order that its visitors can identify with the roles of their ancestors in the shaping of America.

Walter K. Heyer
Executive Director,
Museum of American Frontier Culture,
Staunton, Virginia.

1

Northern *Ireland*

Northern Ireland is an integral part of the United Kingdom with a population of 1.6 million. Its geographical boundary takes in six of the nine counties of the Irish province of Ulster. The majority of the people in Northern Ireland, almost two-thirds, are Protestant and British by culture and tradition, and committed to maintaining the constitutional link with the British Crown.

Just over one-third of the population is Roman Catholic, most of whom are Irish by culture and tradition and seek the reunification of Ireland through a link-up with the Irish Republic. A sizeable number of Roman Catholics in Northern Ireland are known to favour maintaining the status quo link with Britain, therefore it is wrong to look at the political breakdown through a sectarian headcount.

The one million Protestants in Northern Ireland are descendants of Scottish and English settlers who moved from the British mainland in the 17th and 18th centuries. Presbyterians, who formed the bulk of those who moved to the American frontier lands in the 18th century, are today the most numerous Protestant tradition in Northern Ireland, totalling 400,000. The Church of Ireland (Anglican Episcopal) community account for 350,000 people, Methodists 70,000 with smaller Protestant denominations accounting for the rest.

Belfast (population 500,000) is the capital of Northern Ireland and the six counties are Antrim, Down, Londonderry, Tyrone, Armagh and Fermanagh. The main exodus of the Scots-Irish Presbyterians came from four of these counties: Antrim, Down, Tyrone and Londonderry and from Donegal, one of the Ulster counties in the Republic of Ireland.

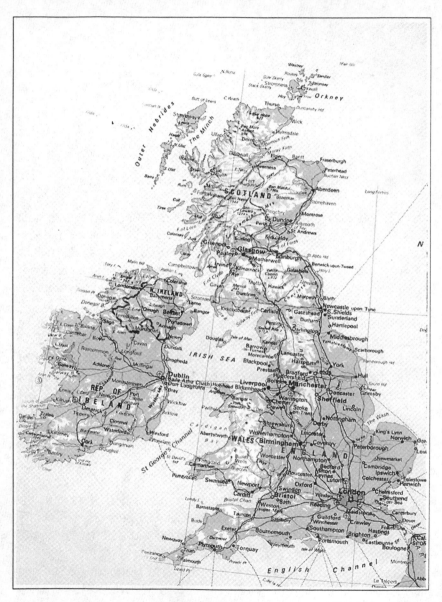

The British Isles

2

Virginia

Virginia, in the north east corner of the Southern region of America, is the oldest of the United States settlements, the state being named for Queen Elizabeth I of England (1533-1603), the Virgin Queen.

The state, running to 40,000 square miles, ranks 36th in size of the 51 American states and today it has a population of almost 5.5 million people. The white sector of the population accounts for 80 per cent of the racial make-up and blacks 19 per cent. The other one per cent consists of native American Indian, Asians and Hispanics.

Richmond (population 220,000) is the capital of Virginia, but Norfolk (population 270,000) is the largest city. Other main population centres are: Virginian Beach (265,000), Arlington (150,000), Newport News (145,000), Hampton (125,000), Chesapeake (115,000), Portsmouth (105,000), Alexandria (105,000) and Roanoke (100,000). Virginia, one of the original 13 colonies, was admitted to the Union on June 26, 1788, the 10th state to ratify the American Constitution.

To the south, Virginia is bordered by North Carolina; in the far west it has a 120-mile border with Kentucky. It also lies adjacent to Tennessee; on the east it fronts on to the Atlantic Ocean. Along the top of its triangular shape, Virginia is bordered by West Virginia to the north west and Maryland and Washington D.C. to the north east.

Virginia, known as the 'Old Dominion State', is very rich in history, being the first permanent English settlement in America, at Jamestown in 1607. It was in Virginia that the British surrendered at the end of the

Revolutionary War and four of the first American Presidents were Virginians, with another four coming later. The first black slaves transported to America arrived in Virginia in 1619 and Richmond was the capital of the Confederacy during the American Civil War of 1861-65. The Confederates also surrendered at Appomattox in Virginia in 1865.

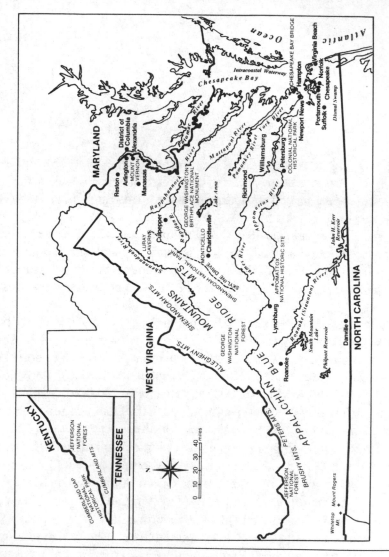

The State of Virginia

O, *Shenandoah*

Shenandoah, an Algonquian word meaning "Daughter of the Stars," is the river in Virginia, but it is both a person and a river in this sea chantey. In the early 19th century the song was solely about a trader in the Missouri River area who fell in love with the daughter of the Algonquian chief Shenandoah. American sailors heading down the Mississippi River took up the slow, rolling melody for the slow, rolling work of hoisting a ship's anchor, changing words to suit their purpose.

O, Shenandoah, I long to hear you
Away, you rolling river
O, Shenandoah, I long to see you
Away, we're bound away
'Cross the wide Missouri.

Oh, Shenandoah, I love your daughter.
Away, you rolling river!
For her I'd cross the rolling water.
Away, I'm bound away, 'cross the wide Missouri.

Oh, Shenandoah, I'm bound to leave you.
Away, you rolling river!
Oh, Shenandoah, I'll not deceive you.
Away, I'm bound away, 'cross the wide Missouri.

"As a race of people, the Scots-Irish were very tough, they were survivor types, who could make good out of a very tough situation. They were eager to do well, there was a real drive there. It always seemed a different kind of drive from the Germans, who settled in the Valley of Virginia at the same time. The Scots-Irish were industrious, ambitious and they were clever, in the sense of being crafty clever in figuring out how to make good of a situation. They have been important in shaping the character of the United States of America and their restless drive in moving on from the settlements of Pennsylvania and Virginia opened up the frontier."

- Dr. Katharine Brown
Museum of Frontier Culture,
Staunton, Virginia

"I can go into Ulster and see the people walking the streets there and return home to Franklin County in Western Virginia and observe an identical looking people. The hats and the coats change, but the looks and the people don't. Three times I have been to Northern Ireland and I have seen the facial characteristics of men and women from these parts. I also see a friendliness in Ulster that I do not see in England or Wales. I see a people eager to talk and help and work with a stranger. I see here and I see there .. I see an independence there that I see here. In looking at home, the likeness with somebody over the hill or a neighbour is uncanny."

- Roddy Moore
Director of Blue Ridge Institute and Museum,
Ferrum, Virginia

★★★

3

Shenandoah - *'daughter of the stars'*

T he word **Shenandoah** comes from the native American language and means "daughter of the stars". It is the title of a beautiful valley of grassland and trees in Virginia that stretches for 200 miles from Lexington north to Harper's Ferry and is bordered on the east by the Blue Ridge Mountains and on the west by the Alleghenies.

The Great Valley of Virginia which includes the Shenandoah Valley was a place of settlement for the Scots-Irish and the Germans during the mid-18th century, but it was also an important commercial route to the west from major population centres like Philadelphia, New Castle, New York and Baltimore.

The settlers who arrived on America's eastern shores from Ulster in the 18th century had two choices if they wanted to move on to the frontier region. They could cross the Allegheny Mountains into western Pennsylvania, but this route brought danger with the native American tribes in no mood to give up their land and hostile to any intrusion by the white settlers. The second option was head south west through Virginia and the Carolina back country and with no settled native population in the Shenandoah Valley and land cheap the route quickly opened up for thousands of families.

The insatiable appetite for land drove the settlers along a moving frontier and the Valley of Virginia was not just a place to put down roots but the through passage to unclaimed territories. The Great Wagon Road, which picked up from the Philadelphia Wagon Road, was extended to the Yadkin River Valley in North Carolina. It was a busy thoroughfare of 450 miles that for upwards of 100 years from 1732 teemed with humanity, hardy souls determined to start a new life on lands they could call their own.

Land was bought and sold for profit, from Pennsylvania to Virginia right through to North Carolina. Some settlers were happy to buy already developed land rather than face the hardships of pioneering in a wilderness. Those who sold and moved on to the edge of the frontier in new states like Tennessee and Kentucky had the money to acquire larger tracts of land at much cheaper prices. More and more the frontier was opened up.

Edmund Burke, in his "Account of the European Settlements" of 1757, wrote: "The number of white people in Virginia is growing every day more numerous by the migration of the Irish, who, not succeeding so well in Pennsylvania as the more frugal and industrious Germans, sell their lands in that province to the latter, and take up new ground in remote countries in Virginia, Maryland and South Carolina. These are chiefly Presbyterians from the northern part of Ireland, who in America were generally called Scotch-Irish".

The first recorded sight of the Shenandoah Valley by a European, John Lederer, was in March, 1670. When, accompanied by an Indian scout, he surveyed the region's hazy blue ridge. Original Indian names and spelling derivations for the Valley may have included Sherando, Genantua, Gerundo and Zynodoa.

German Lutherans were the first immigrants to inhabit the Shenandoah Valley at Massenutten Mountain near Harrisonburg; Winchester (Frederick County region) and at Woodstock (Shenandoah County). They were driven from their homes in the Rhenish Palatinate and Wurtenburg regions of what is today Germany by the ravages of French invaders and the harsh economic conditions prevailing in Europe then. In the early years of the settlements the Germans clung to their own language and stood back from the politics of the region, largely because of their piety and out of loyalty to the then British establishment.

On the heels of the Germans there came to the Great Valley in more numerous numbers a continuing tide of immigrants from the British Isles, much of it made up of Scots-Irish Presbyterians, who were politically active and more adventurous. As soon as the Scots-Irish arrived they quickly moved to secure land grants, sat on the courts and parish councils. In a very short time they were running the place.

In the historical annals of The Southern Appalachians (The Discoverers) it is related that the Scots-Irish, from 1732, followed much the same path as the Germans: "Landing at north eastern ports, they made their way to the hinterlands of New York and Pennsylvania, whence those who could not find land within their means turned south into The Great Valley. Filtering down through the mountains, they met other English and Scots Presbyterians from the Piedmount area of South Carolina, whose experiences of the privileges enjoyed by the Anglican Church and the planter aristocracy had given them a similar rebellious outlook.

"These new Americans were fiercely independent, equalitarian and self-reliant, possessed of an indomitable will to survive and prevail, tough in mind and body. Stung by the slights and injuries they had taken from the advantaged class, their superiors in breeding, cultivation and wealth, they were hostile to all that class stood for. They were bound by no ties to the Old World or like their German fellows, to the English Crown.

"With a stern, fatalistic religion to keep their impetuosity in check, the Scots-Irish combined an intense and ingenious practicality, shrewdness and a long grasp for life's tangibles. From their habituation to clan warfare in the ancestral home and to battling the wild Celts in Ulster, they brought with them a fighting instinct and aggressiveness and a handiness with weapons. Given the nature of the American frontier and the general determination to advance it, regardless, they made ideal frontiersmen, the equal before long of the Redmen, whose woodcraft and dress they adopted. They were not only the new Americans, they were to be the creators of the New America. This would formally succeed to the old when one of their number, Andrew Jackson, was elected to Presidency. And of this New America, which would sweep west-ward to the Pacific in the course of the next century, southern Appalachia was a prime staging area".

Very often the Scots-Irish did not chose the best agricultural lands available to them. The German settlers made the most of the limestone regions, which the Scots-Irish discarded. It was said they preferred slate hills where pure spring water was plentiful, typical of the clean air environment they left behind in the north of Ireland.

Most of the Scots-Irish settlers who arrived in the Shenandoah Valley in the period 1732-60 period stayed put and it was their children and grandchildren who moved west when the lands became scarcer. They did not encounter hostility in the region until the Indian and French wars of 1754-63.

The hitherto uninhabited Shenandoah lands were a paradise to the Scots-Irish settlers, a vast fertile prairie that was both a highly productive and a healthy abode. Indians had used the Valley only as hunting grounds and at the end of each season they set fire to the open ground on the prairie, which ensured it did not develop as woodland. Indians had their sights on buffalo, which lived on grassland and avoided forest.

By their ritual firings the Indian tribes maintained the Shenandoah grassland and all its flowering beauty: dogwood, azalia, rhododendron and laurels. Herds of buffalo, elk and deer roamed freely.

The Scots-Irish settlers adopted many of the Indian ways of farming, hunting and fighting. The "slash, burn and plant" method of toiling the land was used to advantage by the settlers as they dug deep into the Shenandoah soil. Their pattern of life in the backwoods grew closer to that of the native Americans and some historians believe this is what led ultimately to the confrontations that were to follow as more and more land was seized up.

4

Five great waves *of emigration from Ulster*

Between 1717 and the American Revolutionary War years of the late 1770s and early 1780s an estimated quarter of a million Scots-Irish Presbyterian settlers left the Province of Ulster in the northern part of Ireland for the new lands across the Atlantic. They travelled in extremely hazardous conditions, in simple wooden sailing ships from the ports of Belfast, Larne, Londonderry, Newry and Portrush for the far-off berths of Philadelphia, New Castle (Delaware), Charleston, Baltimore and New York.

Huddled together with the most meagre of belongings and money, they were a people forced to move because of the severe restrictions placed on their faith by the ruling British establishment of the day, and because of the economic deprivations prevailing in their Ulster home-land.

The Scots-Irish Presbyterians who headed west 200-250 years ago, belonged to the same race of people who today constitute the majority Protestant and Unionist community in Northern Ireland. Virtually all of these immigrants were so embittered by the discriminatory practices levelled against them by the offices of the Crown that they led the fight against the British in the War of Independence in America.

In Northern Ireland today the Scots-Irish (the Protestant-Unionist population) pledge themselves to the maintenance of the link with Britain, but the complexities of the several hundred years of British history fully explain this paradoxical situation in terms of economic benefit and cultural attachments for the one million people who presently hold firm to this view.

The latter part of the 18th century had seen revolutionary and rebellion against the Crown in Ireland and in America. But in 1801 the Act of Union brought together England, Scotland, Wales and Ireland as one unit under the British Crown and, apart from the breaking away of 26 Irish counties to form the Irish Republic in 1921, the United Kingdom has held closely together since.

In the United States today an estimated 44 million people claim Irish extraction. While the Irish American community, the descendants of the Roman Catholic emigrants who moved at the time of the potato famine in the mid-19th century, are the most vocal and politically active on Ireland, 56 per cent of Americans with Irish roots are of Protestant stock, whose hardy forebears were the Scots-Irish Presbyterians who settled on the frontier in the 18th century.

The first Scots-Irish emigrant ships were chartered in 1717 and in that year, when drought completely ruined the crops on the Ulster farmlands, 5,000 men and women headed to Pennsylvania. The first recorded passenger ship was 'The Friends Goodwill' which left Larne for Boston in April, 1712. There were five great waves of immigration to America from Ulster in the 18th century: 1717-18, 1725-29, 1740-41, 1754-55 and 1771-75.

The migration of 1725-29 was so large that it forced the Government in London to appoint a commission to investigate the causes of movement. Exorbitant rents set by the landlords were cited as the main reason for the second wave; the religious restriction still applied, but poverty had taken its toll and the promise of a better life in the new world proved irresistible.

The Irish famine of 1740-41 led to the third great wave of immigration to America by the Scots-Irish. An estimated 400,000 people perished in that famine and when the Presbyterian settlers arrived in America they set their sights beyond the borders of Pennsylvania - along the path of the Great Valley to the Shenandoah region of Virginia and to South and North Carolina.

The 1754-55 exodus resulted from appeals by colonists in America to settle on the new lands of Virginia and South and North Carolina and from another calamitous drought in Ireland. Thousands headed out, despite a relative improvement in economic conditions back home, and it was during these years that the Scots-Irish came into direct conflict with the native Indian tribes.

In the last great wave of 1771-75, land leases were quoted as the main bone of contention. Not enough ships could be found to carry the throng of Presbyterians eager to go . . . in the two years that followed the evictions in Co. Antrim no fewer than 30,000 Presbyterians left Ulster. It was recorded at the time: "Almost all of them emigrated at their own charge; a great majority of them were persons employed in the linen manufacture or farmers possessed by property which they converted into money and carried with them".

For 50 years after 1775, many more Ulster-Scots emigrated, but the numbers did not match those in the 58 years of the Great Migration.

Next to the English, the Scots-Irish by the end of the 18th century became the most influential section of the white population in America, which, by 1790, numbered 3,172,444. At that time, the Scots-Irish segment of the population totalled about 14 per cent and this figure was much higher in the Appalachian states of Virginia, Tennessee, Kentucky and North Carolina.

In a very short period, the Ulster-Scots and their off-spring progressed from being immigrant settlers to become naturalised Americans, totally assimilated in the fabric of their new nation. Their involvement in the War of Independence made the Scots-Irish think less of their old country and more of the lush fertile lands that were opening up in front of them. As they pioneered the Carolinas, Virginia, and the new states of Kentucky and Tennessee they were increasingly doing so as Americans, not as Irish or Scots.

Those who made the break for the New World did so at a great price. Almost one in three of the Ulster Presbyterians who sailed to America did so under contracts of service or indenture as it was more commonly known. Contracts for terms of between four and seven years were most common and reflected the great need that existed in the colonies for hired help.

The Ulster settlers tended to settle together and mixed little with the English and Germans already there. Poverty also forced them from the more expensive land in the east to the frontier regions, where land was cheap and readily available; others simply squatted in defiance of the authorities.

There were, however, drawbacks, none more so than the risk of being attacked by Indians. Colonial officials were glad to have the Ulster people to provide a defence against hostile natives. When trouble arose, the

Scots-Irish settlers were left to their own devices, an experience which hardened and embittered them against the British Government, just as had been the case back home in Ulster.

It is generally acknowledged that the Revolutionary War for independence in America in the 1770s was essentially a dispute between the Scots-Irish immigrants and the Crown, especially in the Appalachian region. In some Appalachian states in 1776, the Ulster-Scots population was at least one-third.

From Pennsylvania, the Ulster settlement spread along the Valley of Virginia during the 1730s and 1740s following the Great Philadelphia Wagon Road. This was the famous 'backcountry' where their presence was welcomed as a reinforcement against the Indian threat. Most of the movement into North Carolina took place between 1740 and 1756, with the surge into South Carolina developing in the 1760s. The move into East Tennessee developed about 1770-1780.

By the time the Revolutionary War came, about 90 per cent of the Ulster settlers had made their homes in Pennsylvania, the Valley of Virginia and the Carolinas. The Ulster settlers became quite a formidable force. Abandoned to their fate by their British masters, who had let them down so many times in the past, the Ulstermen and women began to feel themselves American above everything else. Ulster families were in the vanguard of the push west. Moving across the mountain barriers, many would leave Virginia for Kentucky, or North Carolina for Tennessee, while many others migrated from eastern Pennsylvania into the Ohio Valley.

President Theodore Roosevelt paid a glowing tribute to this remarkable people: "The backwoodsmen were American by birth and parentage, and of mixed race; but the dominate strain in their blood was that of the Presbyterian-Irish, the Scots-Irish as they were often called. These Irish representatives of the Covenanters were in the west almost what the Puritans were in the north-east, and more than the Cavaliers were in the south. Mingled with the descendants of many other races, they nevertheless formed the kernel of the distinctively and intensely American stock who were the pioneers of our people in their march westward, the vanguard of the army of fighting settlers, who with axe and rifle won their way . . . to the Rio Grande and the Pacific".

5

John Lewis - *Shenandoah's first Scots-Irish settler*

Donegal couple John and Margaret Lewis and their six children are widely acknowledged to be the first immigrants to settle in the southern end of the Shenandoah Valley. In 1732 the Lewises arrived in the region that today is Augusta County with its main town of Staunton and they established a family settlement which more than 260 years on is still very firmly rooted in the rich fertile soil of Virginia.

John Lewis, of Presbyterian stock, was descended from French Huguenots who had moved to Ulster during the mid-17th century. He was born in Donegal in 1678, the son of Andrew and Mary Calhoun Lewis, and his wife Margaret was of the Lynn connection, also a Scots-Irish Presbyterian and from East Donegal close to Londonderry and Lough Foyle. Margaret's brother, Dr. William Lynn, also emigrated to Virginia, settling in Fredericksburg and in his will of 1757 he refers to brothers and sisters living in Strabane (Co. Tyrone) and Letterkenny (Co. Donegal). The Lynns were related to the Pattons of Limavady, who also moved to the American settlements.

Members of the Lewis and Lynn families are believed to have figured on the Protestant Williamite side at the Siege of Londonderry in 1688-89. John Lewis was still a child during this period.

Historical reports relate that John, a tenant farmer of some substance, left Ireland under a cloud after an affray with a landlord who had threatened to dispossess many of his land tenants, including Lewis. In the sharp exchange, the landlord was killed and Lewis hurriedly fled to America, landing in Pennsylvania in 1731.

Mrs. Agatha Towles, a grand-daughter of John Lewis, in a memoir of 1837, states that after his encounter with the landlord he took refuge in a house on "the banks of the Boyne" and as soon as a ship was ready to sail he left for America. Margaret Lewis and her children came on a vessel with 300 passengers, all Presbyterians, and after a journey of three months, landed on the Delaware River.

Within a year he was joined by his wife and young family - four sons Samuel, Thomas, Andrew and William and two daughters Margaret and Anne. A fifth son Charles was born in Augusta County four years after their arrival. The Lewises came to the Shenandoah Valley as an isolated family before careful attempts were made to settle the region as part of the Beverley Manor. They had trudged most of the journey on foot, trekking along an old buffalo trail used by the Indians.

There are no reports that John Lewis was ever charged for the alleged misdemeanour in Ireland although he must have received some form of pardon. He never returned to his Donegal homeland and stories about involvement in the killing of a landlord have been given various slants by historians in America down the years.

Whatever the true nature of the incident, John Lewis and his family prospered in America after a few tough years acclimatising to the wilds of the frontier. He built his Irish-style Fort Lewis home - a half stone, half log cabin structure - at Bellefonte about two miles east of present-day Staunton and with his four sons set about immediately to till the lush Shenandoah lands. The Lewises were assisted in the settlement by an aristocrat of English stock, Sir William Beverley, who was heavily involved at the time in land speculation in Virginia.

Beverley, in 1736, acquired 118,491 acres of land in the shadow of the Blue Ridge Mountains close to the Shenadoah River and in the several years from the arrival of the Lewis family about 60 families of Scots-Irish vintage moved into the region. These settlers squatted at first in clearings they had opened up with their own hands, but eventually bought the holdings from Beverley.

Additional settlers were attracted to Staunton along the Great Wagon Road when Beverley circulated notices in Pennsylvania and hired an Ulster sea captain James Patton, from Limavady, Co. Londonderry, to entice the ever-increasing flow of immigrants and indentures from the north of Ireland. Within a decade so many Scots-Irish families had settled on Beverley's lands that it became widely known as the Irish Tract, with Staunton a town of much Scots-Irish influence.

Patton, who served in the Royal Navy, had his own ship and is reported to have crossed the Atlantic 25 times, carrying cargoes of goods, and hundreds of Ulstermen and women. Patton was related to John and Margaret Lewis by way of his mother's Lynn connection.

Augusta County was formally organised in 1745, with Thomas Lewis, son of the first settler, appointed county surveyor and Captain James Patton sheriff. With Orange County, which had been organised in 1734, Augusta County stretched from the Blue Ridge Mountains to the frontier limits of Virginia, bordering on so-far largely unpopulated territories like Kentucky, Ohio, Indiana, Illinois and western Pennsylvania.

Until the Scots-Irish settlers moved in, the valley of Virginia had lain largely uninhabited. The native Indian tribes passed through the region and hunted there, but they had not settled villages. Relationships between the settlers and Indians in the early years were friendly but guarded. Tensions, however, surfaced after 1750 when the pioneers began crossing the Allegheny Mountains to take up Indian lands and hostilities started that were to become known as the French and Indian Wars. Andrew and Charles Lewis, sons of the first settler, participated in this conflict.

John Lewis, for the bargain price of fourteen pounds, acquired the title for 2,071 acres of Beverley Manor land in 1739. But William Beverley explained the favour was bestowed on Lewis "for the extraordinary trouble of his house and charges in entertaining those who had come to settle on Beverley Manor". It was located in the vicinity of the twin hills "Betsy Bell" and "Mary Gray", which were named by the settlers after two similar hills in the Sperrins region of Co. Tyrone.

The Lewis home was a meeting place and social centre for the new settlers. It was there that the Rev. James Anderson, who had been sent to Virginia by the Presbyterian Synod of Philadelphia, preached in 1738 what was the first regular sermon ever delivered in this part of the American frontier.

The new settlers were arriving daily, some on horseback or by mule-drawn carts along what were nothing more than dirt tracks. Much later settlers came in the horse-drawn Conestoga covered wagons which were a familiar sight in the opening up of the west in the early 19th century. From 1750 to 1776, it was said that the southbound settlers heading along the Great Wagon Road were numbered in tens of thousands.

John Lewis was a highly ambitious pioneer and not only did he enjoy the reputation of being the first settler in the southwest Shenandoah Valley, but he was the most influential during the middle part of the 18th century.

His five sons and two daughters sustained the family influence: Thomas surveyed the Fairfax Line, which forms the northern boundary of Rockingham County and part of Virginia's borders with West Virginia, he also laid out the formal plan of the town of Staunton in 1747-48 and by the end of his life was the largest landowner in Rockingham, County, Virginia. Thomas was also a member of the Virginia Convention; Andrew, a close associate of George Washington, became the region's most prominent military leader, defeating the Indians at Point Pleasant on the Ohio River, becoming a brigadier general in the Continental army, and commanding the Virginian troops at the defence of Williamsburg.

William, a pious Covenanting Presbyterian and church elder, moved to West Virginia, where his family developed the region's valuable mineral deposits, while American-born Charles died at the Battle of Point Pleasant, after heroics as a frontiersman and militia soldier. William Irvine Lewis, a grandson of William, died with Davy Crockett at the Alamo in 1836, while many of the Lewises lost their lives on both sides in the American Civil War.

Margaret Lewis, John Lewis's elder daughter, settled in Kentucky, while Anne moved back to Pennsylvania. Members of the Lewis family were among the first to settle in Georgia, Tennessee, Kentucky, Texas and Utah and astronaut Edward H. White 11, a descendant of Andrew Lewis, became the first American to walk in space.

Other descendants were: John Francis Lewis (1895), the United States Senator for Virginia and twice Lieutenant Governor of Virginia; George Rockingham Gilmer, a first lieutenant in the war against the Creek Indians in 1813 and twice Governor of Georgia, and Charles Spittal Robb, the Governor of Virginia in the 1980s.

John Lewis, the first southern Shenandoah settler, died at Bellefonte on February 1, 1762, aged 84. His wife Margaret died 11 years later, aged 80. Both were exceptional people who courageously blazed a trail along the American frontier that was to be a shining inspiration to thousands of their kinsfolk who headed along a similar path.

• The epitaph on the grave of John Lewis at Staunton reads: "Here lies the remains of John Lewis, born in Donegal County, Ireland in 1678, who slew the Irish lord, settled Augusta County, located the town of Staunton and furnished five sons to fight the battle of the American Revolution. He was a brave man, a true patriot and a friend of liberty throughout the world".

A passage from the notes of Thomas Lewis, the surveyor, illustrates the kind of hardships the early pioneers experienced in the Shenandoah Valley:

"This River was Calld Styx from the Dismal apperance of the place Being Sufficen to Strick terror in any human Creature [;] ye Lorels [laurels] Ivey * Spruce pine so Extremly thick in ye Swamp through which this River Runs that one Cannot have the Least prospect Except they look upwards[.] the Water of the River of Dark Brownish Cooler & its motion So Slow that it can hardly be Siad to move [.] its Depth about 4 feet the Bottom muddy & Banks high which made it Extremely Difficult for us to pass [.] the most of the horses when they attempt'd to asend the farthest Bank tumbling with their loads Back in the River. most of our Bagage that would have been Damaged by the water were Brought over on mens Shoulder Such as Powder, Bread and Bedclothes &c ... we Could not find a plain Bieg enough for one man to Lye on no fire wood Except green or Roten Spruce pine [,] no place for our horses to feed [.] And to prevent their Eating of Loral tyd them all up least they Should be poisoned."[1]

[1] The Fairfax Line by John W. Wayland 1925.

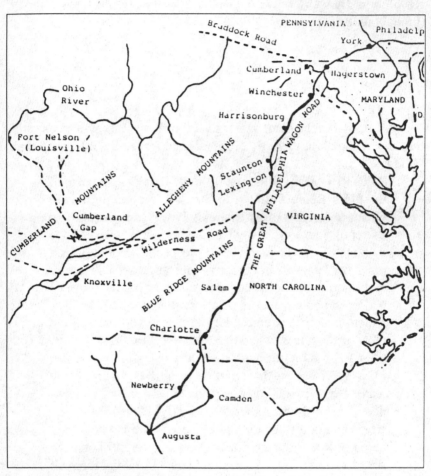

The Great Philadelphia Wagon Road

6

The Scots-Irish *and the Declaration of Independence*

T homas Jefferson, a Virginian of English stock, drafted the American Declaration of Independence in 1776 and at least eight of the 56 signatories of the Declaration Scots-Irish. The Declaration, signed in Philadelphia on July 4, 1776, was a statement which enshrined much of the independent and democratic spirit of the Presbyterian settlers from Ulster.

The man who transcribed the document was Charles Thompson, a native of Maghera in Co. Londonderry. Thompson held the high rank of Perpetual Secretary to the Continental Congress in America, the legislature which was then the alternative ruling body to the Crown. The house at Upperlands outside Maghera where Charles Thompson lived is marked with a memorial plaque.

Of the eight Scots-Irish signators, John Hancock from Massachusetts is undoubtedly the best known. He was the President of Congress and his signature on the Declaration was not only the first but the largest. It was reputed that King George III had bad eyesight and Hancock wrote large to make sure his name was not missed. On completing his signature, Hancock, of Banbridge, Co. Down extraction, said: "There, I guess King George will be able to read that".

The other seven known Scots-Irishmen who signed the famous document were:

• William Whipple - his parents had arrived in Maine from Ireland in 1730.

• Robert Paine- his grandfather came from Dungannon, Co. Tyrone.
• Thomas McKean - his father came from Ballymoney, Co. Antrim.
• Thomas Nelson - his grandfather came from Strabane, Co. Tyrone.
• Matthew Thornton - from Londonderry, he settled in New Hampshire in 1718.
• George Taylor - the son of an Ulster Presbyterian minister.
• Edward Rutledge - another son of an Ulster Presbyterian family.

After being transcribed, debated and signed by the Continental Congress, the Declaration was then passed on to another native-born Ulsterman for printing. John Dunlap had moved from a printing company in Strabane, Co. Tyrone to work in America in the mid-18th century and it fell on him the honour of printing the first copies of the Declaration. Later in 1784, Dunlap had the distinction of printing America's first daily newspaper, The Pennsylvania Packet. Soon after it was signed the Declaration was widely distributed throughout America, with the first public reading being enacted by Colonel John Nixon, whose father was also Ulster-born.

7

Virginian trail *to the Presidency*

Virginia has provided more Presidents of the United States than any other state of the Union. Eight Virginians made it to the White House, including Woodrow Wilson who was of Scots-Irish Presbyterian descent - his grandfather James Wilson emigrated to Philadelphia in 1807 from Strabane in Co. Tyrone.

The eight Virginian Presidents were:

• George Washington, born Washington County, Virginia. Religion - Episcopalian. Republican President 1789-1797.

• Thomas Jefferson, born Goochland now Albermarle County, Virginia. Religion - Episcopalian. Republican President 1801-09.

• James Madison, born King George County, Virginia. Religion - Episcopalian. Republican President 1809-1817.

• James Monroe, born Westmoreland County, Virginia. Religion - Episcopalian. Republican President 1817-1825.

• William Henry Harrison, born Charles County, Virginia. Religion - Episcopalian. Republican President 1840-1841.

• John Tyler, born Charles County, Virginia. Religion - Episcopalian. Republican President 1841-1845.

• Zachary Taylor, born Orange County, Virginia. Religion - Episcopalian. Republican President 1848-1850.

• Woodrow Wilson, born Staunton, Virginia. Religion - Presbyterian. Democrat President 1913-1921.

The other states who provided Presidents were:

• Ohio 7 - Ulysses S. Grant (Republican 1869-1877. Religion - Methodist); Rutherford B. Hayes (Republican 1877-1881. Religion - Presbyterian); James A. Garfield (Republican March 4 - September 19, 1881. Religion - Disciples of Christ); Benjamin Harrison (Republican 1889-1893. Religion - Presbyterian); William McKinley (Republican 1897-1901. Religion - Methodist); William Howard Taft (Republican 1909-1913. Religion - Unitarian); Warren G. Harding (Republican 1921-23. Religion - Baptist).

• Massachusetts 4 - John Adams (Republican 1797-1801. Religion - Unitarian); John Quincy Adams (Republican - 1825-1829. Religion - Unitarian); John F. Kennedy (Democrat 1961-1963. Religion - Roman Catholic); George Bush (Republican 1989-1993. Religion - Episcopalian).

• New York 4 - Martin Van Buren (Democrat 1837-1841. Religion - Episcopalian); Millard Fillmore (Republican 1850-1853. Religion - Unitarian); Theodore Roosevelt (Republican 1901-1909. Religion - Dutch Reformed Church). Franklin D. Roosevelt (Democrat 1933-1945. Religion - Episcopalian).

• Tennessee 3 - Andrew Jackson (Democrat 1829-1837. Religion - Presbyterian); James K. Polk (Democrat 1845-1849. Religion - Presbyterian); Andrew Johnson (Democrat 1865-1869. Religion - Presbyterian).

• Vermont 2 - Chester Alan Arthur (Republican 1881-1885. Religion - Episcopalian); Calvin Coolidge (Republican 1923-1929. Religion - Congregationalist).

• Texas 2 - Dwight D. Eisenhower (Republican 1954-1961. Religion - Presbyterian); Lyndon B. Johnson (Democrat 1963-1969. Religion - Disciples of Christ).

• New Hampshire 1 - Franklin Pierce (Democrat 1853-1857. Religion - Episcopalian).

• Pennsylvania 1 - James Buchanan (Democrat 1857-1861. Religion - Presbyterian).

• Kentucky 1 - Abraham Lincoln (Republican 1861-1865. Religion - Presbyterian).

• New Jersey 1 - Grover Cleveland (Democrat 1885-1889 and 1893-97. Religion - Presbyterian).

• Illinois 1 - Ronald Reagan (Republican 1981-1989. Religion - Presbyterian).

• Iowa 1 - Herbert Hoover (Republican 1923-1933. Religion - Quaker).

• Missouri 1 - Harry S. Truman (Democrat 1945-1954. Religion - Baptist).

• California 1 - Richard M. Nixon (Republican 1969-1974. Religion - Quaker).

• Nebraska 1 - Gerald R. Ford (Republican 1974-1977. Religion - Episcopalian).

• Georgia 1 - Jimmy Carter (Democrat 1977-1981. Religion - Baptist).

• Arkansas 1 - Bill Clinton (Democrat 1993-1996. Religion - Baptist).

Eleven of the 41 Presidents of the United States can definitely trace their direct ancestry back to the Ulster-Scots families who moved to the American frontier 200-250 years ago. Three - Andrew Jackson, James Buchanan and Chester Alan Arthur - came from first generation parents. Jackson was born 18 months after his parents left Boneybefore outside Carrickfergus in 1765.

The American Presidents with firmly established Ulster links are:

• Andrew Jackson: (Democrat - 7th President, 1829-37). Born on March 15, 1767 in the Waxhaw region of North Carolina, his family had left Ulster in 1765, having lived in the village of Boneybefore near Carrickfergus. Andrew helped draft the constitution for Tennessee, which became the 16th state of Union, on June 1, 1796. Jackson was a lawyer, soldier and politician and not only did he fight in the Revolutionary War, as a teenager, but was the man who quelled the native Indian revolts in the early 19th century. His wife Rachel was a daughter of John Donelson, a founder of the city of Nashville and another of East Co. Antrim roots. He was a Presbyterian.

• James Knox Polk: (Democrat - 11th President, 1845-49). Born on November 2, 1795 near Charlotte in North Carolina, he is descended from a Robert Polk (Polok) of Londonderry, who had arrived in the American colonies about 1680. Was a Governor of Tennessee, Speaker of the House of Representatives in Washington, and a President who was successful in carrying out all of the major policies he set out to implement. Polk and his wife Sarah are buried in the State Capital in Nashville. During his life, Polk was both a Presbyterian and a Methodist. He died four months after his term as President.

• James Buchanan: (Democrat - 15th President, 1857-61). Born on April 23, 1791 in Mercersburg, Pennsylvania, he was born into a Presbyterian home like his predecessors Jackson and Polk. The family came originally from Deroran near Omagh and left Donegal for America in 1783. Buchanan, described as an imposing handsome figure, was the United States Minister to Russia (in 1832-33) and Britain (in 1853-56) and was Secretary of State during James K. Polk's Presidency. Buchanan was a Presbyterian.

• Andrew Johnson: (Democrat - 17th President, 1865-69). Born on December 29, 1808 in Raleigh, North Carolina, his namesake and grandfather from Mounthill outside Larne had come to America about 1750, from the port of Larne. He rose to the Presidency from humble log cabin origins and worked as a tailor for many years in the Tennessee town of Greeneville. He was Mayor of Greeneville, Governor of Tennessee, a United States Governor, Military Governor of Tennessee during the American Civil War, and was elected Vice-President to Abraham Lincoln in 1865. When Lincoln was assassinated shortly into his Presidency, Johnson assumed the office, but he became highly unpopular with his Southern voters when he backed the Union cause. Johnson's family were originally Presbyterian, but he worshipped both as a Methodist and Baptist.

• Ulysses Simpson Grant: (Republican - 18th President, 1869-77). The man who commanded the Union Army in the American Civil War, his mother Hannah Simpson was descended from the Simpson family of Dergenagh near Dungannon. His great grandfather John Simpson had left Ulster for America in 1760. Grant, a Methodist, fought in the Mexican War and rose from second lieutenant to general in the Civil War. Grant was essentially a soldier and, although he took no part in the 1868 Presidential campaign, there was such a momentum for peace in the country that he won the popular vote with the theme: "Let us have peace".

• Chester Alan Arthur: (Republican - 21st President, 1881-85). Born on October 5, 1829 in Fairfield, Vermont, his grandfather and father, Baptist pastor William Arthur, emigrated to the United States from Dreen near Cullybackey in Co. Antrim in 1801. Arthur's people were Presbyterian, but he worshipped as an Episcopalian. He was Collector at the Port of New York for seven years and was Vice-President to James A. Garfield from March to September, 1881. When Garfield was assassinated, Arthur took over. Before entering politics, he was a school teacher and a lawyer.

• Grover Cleveland: (Democrat - 22nd and 24th President 1885-89 and 1893-97). Born on March 18, 1837, in Caldwell, New Jersey, his maternal grandfather Abner Neal had left County Antrim in the late 18th century. Son of a Presbyterian minister, Cleveland was at 250 pounds, one of the heaviest of the American Presidents. He was a lawyer and a sheriff of Erie County in New York in 1871-73; Mayor of Buffalo, New York in 1882 and Governor of New York in 1883-85. He served two Presidential terms, defeating Republican Benjamin Harrison, the man who succeeded him in 1889, on the second time round.

• Benjamin Harrison: (Republican - 23rd President, 1889-93). Born on August 20, 1833 at North Bend, Ohio, two of his great grandfathers James Irwin and William McDowell were Ulstermen. Another Presbyterian, Harrison fought in the Civil War on the Union side with the 17th Indiana Infantry Regiment and rose from second lieutenant to brigadier general. He was a lawyer in Indianapolis and was a leading supporter of President Abraham Lincoln. He served as a United States Senator from 1881 to 1887.

• William McKinley: (Republican - 25th President, 1897-1901). Born on January 29, 1843 in Niles, Ohio, he was the great grandson of James McKinley, who had emigrated to America from Conagher, near Ballymoney in County Antrim about 1743. McKinley was a Methodist, although he was married in a Presbyterian Church. He served in the Civil War with the 23rd Ohio Volunteer Infantry, rising from private to major. He became a lawyer and was United States representative for Ohio for 12 years and Governor of Ohio from 1892 to 1896. At the start of his second term as President, McKinley was assassinated at Buffalo, New York - on September 6, 1901.

• Woodrow Wilson: (Democrat - 28th President, 1913-21). Born on December 18, 1856 in Staunton, Virginia he was the grandson of James Wilson who had emigrated from Dergalt near Strabane in County Tyrone about 1807. His father, Dr. Joseph Ruggles Wilson was a Presbyterian minister. Wilson taught political economy and public law at Bryn Mawr in Pennsylvania College and was professor of history at Wesleyan University in Middletown, Connecticut, before moving to Princeton University where he became president. He was Governor of New Jersey for two years leading up to the Presidency. As President during the First World War, Wilson was heavily involved in top-level discussions with other world leaders. He was considered one of the greatest Presidents in American history.

• Richard Milhouse Nixon: (Republican - 37th President, 1969-74). Born on January 13, 1913 in Yorba Linda, California, he has Ulster connections on two sides of his family. His Nixon ancestor left County Antrim and County Fermanagh for America about 1753 and settled in Castle County, Delaware, while the Milhouses, a Quaker family, came from Carrickfergus and Ballymoney. Nixon was a Quaker himself, but attended services of other denominations and rejected the Quaker tenet of pacifism, enlisting in the Navy in the Second World War. He was a United States Senator for two years in 1951-53 and Vice-President for the two Presidential terms of Dwight D. Eisenhower. Although his own Presidential career was tarnished by the Watergate scandal, Nixon is credited with being an excellent President on American foreign policy, particularly in relations with the Communist eastern bloc. He resigned in 1974 over the Watergate scandal and died in 1994.

• A grandfather of President Bill Clinton (1993-) five times removed was Lucas Cassidy, who left Rosslea in Co. Fermanagh for America around 1750, it is claimed. A scroll bearing testimony to President Clinton's membership of the Clan Cassidy is displayed at the Oval Office. The President, who visited Northern Ireland in November, 1995, has strongly emphasised his Ulster roots since coming to the White House. Lucas Cassidy would have been of Presbyterian stock.

8

Woodrow Wilson - *US President from Staunton*

S on of a Presbyterian minister, Thomas Woodrow Wilson and third generation Ulster/Scot was considered to be one of America's most distinguished Presidents. The man who successfully guided the United States through the First World War was a Virginian by his Staunton, Augusta County birth in 1856, although he only spent the first year of his life in the Shenandoah Valley. The family moved to Augusta in Georgia and eventually to South Carolina, and North Carolina for the rest of his childhood years.

Woodrow Wilson had warm Ulster and Scottish blood in his veins: his paternal grandfather James Wilson emigrated from North Tyrone in 1807, while his maternal grandfather the Rev. Thomas Woodrow was a native of Paisley in Scotland, moving to America in 1835 to take a Presbyterian congregation charge in Ohio.

Strabane man James Wilson was 20 when he headed from the nearby port of Londonderry to Philadelphia. He had grown up in the rural hamlet of Dergelt, about two miles from Strabane and in the foothills of the Sperrin Mountains, and he had just completed his apprenticeship as a printer at Gray's Shop at Bridge Street, Strabane when he moved. Remains of the humble Wilson homestead at Dergelt are still preserved to this day and descendants of the original family reside in the Strabane area.

Gray's printing shop was an establishment of note, for it was there that John Dunlap, who printed the American Declaration of Independence in 1776 and who founded the first American daily newspaper The

Pennsylvania Packet, was apprenticed. The close connection between Gray's and America provided opportunity for James Wilson because John Dunlap was still alive when he arrived in Philadelphia in 1807 and the Ulster link was sustained.

James Wilson found employment on the Democratic newspaper The Aurora and within five years he had gained control of the paper, fiercely espousing the Democratic ideals of Benjamin Franklin. He moved to Ohio and became editor of the Western Herald and Gazette in Steubenville, as well as taking on the mantle of Democratic politics in the state legislature and law as assistant judge at the Court of Common Pleas.

His wife Anne Adams was also Ulster-born, but exactly where has not been positively verified. Some historians point to Donaghadee along the north Co. Down coastline as her homeland, other sources claim Sion Mills near Strabane as the more likely locality. Anne Adams is said to have told her children that she lived on the coast of Ulster, so near that she could see the linen drying on the lines in Scotland across the channel. If this is correct, Donaghadee, with its very close proximity to Scotland, would have been her home.

In 1808, Anne Adams married James Wilson in Fourth Philadelphia Presbyterian Church and the couple had 10 children - seven sons and three daughters. The youngest and seventh son of seven sons, Joseph Ruggles Wilson became a scholarly Presbyterian minister and his third child was President Woodrow Wilson. The President's mother was Jessie Woodrow from Carlisle in England, who had emigrated to America with her family when she was only four.

President Wilson often spoke of his Scots-Irish background, claiming with great pride that he had inherited the stern, strongly independent characteristics of the Scottish Covenanters. Speaking at a St. Patrick's Day rally in New York in 1909, when he was President of Princeton University, Woodrow Wilson said: "I myself am happy that there runs in my veins a very considerable strain of Irish blood. I can't prove it from documents, but I have internal evidence. There is something delightful in me that every now and then takes the strain off my Scotch conscience and affords me periods of most enjoyable irresponsibility when I do not care whether school keeps or not or whether anybody gets educated or not".

In 1913, a year after he was elected to his first term as a Democratic President, Wilson said: "I am sorry to say that my information about my father's family is very meagre. My father's father was born in the North of Ireland, he had no brothers on this side of the water. The family came from the neighbourhood, I have understood as Londonderry".

President Wilson visited Ireland in August 1899, taking in both the north and south of the island. He is understood to have made it to Belfast, but the only evidence of his trip is in a letter located amongst his personal papers. This was written on August 20 from the White Horse Inn at Drogheda in Co. Louth, about 25 miles from the present Irish border.

He wrote: "Crowds both on board the boat from England and in Dublin for the Dublin Horse Show have decided me to make my journey northward at once and by rail, asking chance acquaintances on the boat where I should go to; and therefore I am in Drogheda. I don't clearly know yet exactly where Drogheda is. I have not been able to find a map to look it up on. I only know that it is north of Dublin, some 30 or 40 miles and somehow on the way to Belfast. But it's not on me to repine just now. This is the last letter before I come myself. I sail Saturday".

Wilson at the time was professor of jurisprudence and political economy at Princeton University and apart from contacts in the academic world, few in Ireland would have been aroused by his 1899 visit. He knew little about the geography of Ireland and he would not have reached North Tyrone to trace his grandfather's roots.

President Wilson's 1913-21 Presidential term coincided with the years of the bitter political struggle in Ireland, but despite intense pressure on him from Irish-American elements within the Democratic Party to intervene on behalf of the Irish nationalist cause the President wisely did not get involved.

He saw the Irish situation purely as an internal British matter and did not perceive the dispute and the unrest in Ireland as comparable to the plight of the various nationalities in Europe as a result of the fall-out from the First World War. He ignored a letter from Irish nationalist leaders in Dublin in 1918 calling on the United States to back moves for the disengagement of British interests in Ireland. The nationalist letter was countered by a communique from Ulster Unionist leaders in the North, including Lord Edward Carson, but the President was unmoved that American involvement was required.

Woodrow Wilson was considered an emotionally complex man, one who craved affection and demanded unquestioned loyalty. He once described his nature as a struggle between his Irish blood - "quick, generous, impulsive, passionate, anxious always to help and to sympathise with those in distress" and his Scotch blood "canny, tenacious and perhaps a little exclusive".

Paradoxically, he was, before large crowds supremely self-confident and a gifted moving orator; with small groups of strangers he was often shy and awkward. He was married twice, first to Ellen Louise Axson, from Savannah, Georgia and after her death 29 years into the marriage he wed widower Mrs. Edith Bolling Galt, who survived him by 37 years. Throughout her life Ellen Louise Axson Wilson had a deep and abiding interest in art and her father had also been a Presbyterian minister.

Religion was Woodrow Wilson's driving force and he said his life would not be worth living were it not for faith, pure and simple. "I have seen all my life the arguments against it without ever having been moved by them. Never for a moment have I had one doubt about my religious beliefs", he asserted. Wilson read his Bible daily in the White House, said grace before meals and prayed on his knees each morning and night. He belonged to Central Presbyterian Church in Washington and regularly attended the midweek prayer meetings. He firmly believed in providence and predestination and that God had foreordained him as President. His Calvinistic upbringing remained with him throughout his life.

Woodrow Wilson was a college lecturer in the years up to the end of the 19th century, teaching in Pennsylvania and Connecticut before taking the chair in jurisprudence and political economy at Princeton University. In 1902 he became the first layman to head Princeton, an institution founded by Scots-Irish Presbyterian clerics. He held this position until 1910.

He became Governor of New Jersey in 1911 after being persuaded to run by the Democratic bosses, who realised this was a man with the political acumen to go the whole way to the White House. A Presidential election loomed ahead and Wilson began his campaign for the nomination on a speaking tour of the West in 1911. The following year he won the nomination and on November 5, 1912 was elected with a 42 per cent popular vote (6,286,820) over Theodore Roosevelt, who had 27 per cent (4,126,020) and the outgoing Republican President William Howard Taft on 23 per cent (3,483,922). Wilson carried the electoral vote in 40 states.

Four years later the Wilson bandwagon was again successful - he had a 49 per cent poll (9,129,606) over Republican Charles Evans Hughes, who had 46 per cent (8,538,221). On this occasion his electoral college majority was slimmer: 277-254.

His 1912 campaign centred on the 'New Freedom' manifesto, and a pledge to end monopoly, restore free competition and establish the right of labour to bargain collectively for its welfare. The war in Europe dominated the 1916 campaign and the Democrats carried the slogan: "He kept us out of War". It was a close-run thing, however, especially when Theodore Roosevelt backed the Republican candidate over greater US involvement in the War and Roman Catholic voters moved against Wilson over his hostile attitude to Roman Catholic-dominated Mexico, then in the middle of a bloody revolution.

At the outset of the War in 1914 Wilson advised that the United States should remain strictly neutral, but American opinion gradually changed after incidents of German hostility, including the sinking of the British liner Lusitania off the southern coast of Ireland which claimed 1,200 lives, including 120 American passengers. The natural affinity of many Americans also brought the United States closer to involvement in the War, but it was not until April, 1917 that they were officially engaged.

American reinforcements were enough to tip the balance in the War towards the Allied Command, yet when the Armistice was signed on November 11, 1918 more than 300,000 Americans had been killed. Woodrow Wilson led the American delegation at the Paris Peace Conference and he played a leading part in drawing up the Treaty of Versailles of 1919, which placed full blame for the war on Germany. The League of Nations was formed as a result of the peace deliberations.

By the end of 1919 Woodrow Wilson was exhausted and he suffered a stroke from which he never fully recovered. For his efforts in achieving world peace and forming the League of Nations, the President was awarded the Nobel Peace Prize. Under Wilson's leadership, America had become a world power, industry and commerce flourished across the States and the nation's stability was maintained until the depression emerged a decade later.

Woodrow Wilson bowed out as President on March 4, 1921 and his retirement lasted only three years. He died on February 3, 1924 aged 67, and had no state funeral, preferring a simple service in his home. He is the only President buried in Washington.

As a President, Woodrow Wilson ranks amongst the greats, and it was another occupant of the White House, Herbert Hoover who paraphrased this tribute: "Three qualities stood out in Woodrow Wilson. He was a man of staunch morals. He was more than just an idealist; he was the personification of the heritage of idealism of the American people. He brought spiritual concepts to the peace table, he was a born crusader".

Woodrow Wilson was in the highest tradition of the Scots-Irish, a President who advanced American prestige and honour throughout the world. His patriotism, idealism and Christian faith were an inspiration to the free world.

• The life and Presidential career of Woodrow Wilson is remembered at a memorial museum in Staunton, Virginia, the town of his birth. It is sited in the manse, where his father the Rev. Joseph Ruggles Wilson had moved to with his family in March, 1855 when he accepted a call from the congregation of First Staunton Presbyterian Church. The museum contains, among other personal belongings of the Wilson family, the Bible in which the Rev. Wilson recorded the birth of his son Woodrow "at 123/4 o'clock at night" on December 28, 1856.

• The father of President Abraham Lincoln, Thomas Lincoln was born at Lacey Spring, Rockingham County, Virginia in 1778. The Lincolns were an English family and moved to Kentucky, where Abraham was born in 1809.

• Texas-born President, Dwight D. Eisenhower came of German settlers who moved to the Shenandoah Valley in the 1730s. It is firmly believed that his great-great-great-grandfather was Jacob Stover, who led the German settlers down the Warriors' Path in Virginia in 1726. The President's mother Ida Stover was born in the Fort Defiance area of Augusta County in 1862. The Rev. John Casper Stover (Jun) was the first German Lutheran minister to preach in the Shenandoah Valley, about 1732.

9

The spirit of Calvinism *in the Shenandoah*

Augusta and Rockbridge Counties in the Shenandoah Valley are said to be the most Scots-Irish populated regions in the present-day United States and it is there that Presbyterians abound in numbers more numerous than any other denomination. In the first settlements of those counties the Scots-Irish numbered two thirds of the population. (1)

The spirit of Calvinism that was taken from lowland Scotland to the north of Ireland was cradled in the Valley of Virginia by families who brought with them on the long arduous trek across the Atlantic their Bibles, their Catechisms and their Confession of Faith. One such family was the Doaks, who had left the hillsides of Co. Antrim in the dreadful winter of 1739-40 - "the time of the black frost" - to start a new life on the American frontier.

The Rev. Samuel Doak was the son of one of five brothers from Ballynure in Co. Antrim who moved from Pennsylvania through to Virginia in 1740 and he became the most acclaimed cleric on the American revolutionary side during the War of Independence in the 1770s and early 1780s.

The Rev. Samuel Doak was born in Augusta County on August 1, 1749, nine years after his parents arrived in the region. His father Samuel had settled in the area with his four brothers John, Nathaniel, Robert and David and two sisters Ann and Thankful. Samuel Sen. married Jane Mitchell, a widow with three children known to him back in their Ulster homeland, and their Christian piety greatly influenced young Samuel from an early age.

Growing up for Samuel Doak was a hazardous and laborious exist-ence; he worked dawn to dusk on the family farm as a child and lived daily with the threat of Indian attack, something that stuck with him long into his adult marital years when he moved to live in East Tennes-see.

Augusta County records show that Samuel and Jane Doak possessed a deed of land near Staunton in September, 1741, almost a decade on from Co. Donegal man John Lewis first arrived to settle in the area. The Doaks were part of the large influx of immigrants who had moved along the Great Philadelphia Wagon Road; Ulster-Scots and some Germans, and gradually Augusta and Rockbridge Counties took root.

The Rev. John Craig arrived in Augusta in 1740 to become the first Presbyterian minister to settle in Western Virginia. He had been sent by the Donegal Presbytery in Pennsylvania after a petition had been re-ceived from the Presbyterian settlers in the Valley of Virginia. Craig organised the Augusta Stone Church and the Tinkling Spring Church and he had a congregation which stretched for 30 square miles.

Presbyterian clergymen were assured they would not suffer "inter-ruption" in their services so long as they "conform themselves to the rules prescribed by the Act of Toleration in taking the oaths of loyalty to the Crown and the Protestant religion, and registering the places of their meeting and behave themselves peaceably towards the Government (in London)".

In the early years of Virginian settlements until the Revoluntionary War, the Episcopal Church was the only officially recognised church in the state and although perhaps half of the people belonged to other de-nominations, everyone was taxed to pay the salaries of Anglican clerics. This tariff was loosely observed in parts of the Shenandoah where the Scots-Irish Presbyterians were in large numbers. Effectively, the writ of the Anglican church did not run west of the Allegheny Mountains and few if any clerics of this denomination had a presence in the Blue Ridge/ Shenandoah Valley region until the early 19th century.

The Doaks attended the New Providence Presbyterian Church which was founded by a Rev. John Blair, who, along with ministerial colleagues, was responsible for setting up 23 Presbyterian churches in the Shenandoah Valley. The families of New Providence were said to "keep the Sabbath with great strictness, and family worship was almost uni-versal".

Historian Dr. William Henry Foote, who compiled 'Sketches of Virginia, Historical and Biographical', wrote of the settlers' loyalty to their church: "Tradition along the frontier says the first work after building log cabins for themselves, was to erect a capacious meeting house. For permanency and dignity they determined it should be of stone. Limestone for mortar could be found in abundance, but sand was brought on pack-horses, six and seven miles from the stream called South Fork. Nails and glass were brought in the same way from Philadelphia that their house of worship should be properly finished, that they forebore not only luxuries, but what are esteemed the necessaries of housewifery. One old lady apologised to some company that came to eat with her, for not accommodating more at a time at the table and requiring them to eat by turns, that all might have the benefit of the few knives and forks. She said: 'We intended to have got a set of knives this year, but the meeting house was to be finished, and we could not give our share and get the knives, so we put them off for another'." Such was the sacrifice for one's faith along the frontier.

The Doaks were a God-fearing people and early in his teens young Samuel began studies for the ministry, both in Virginia and in Maryland. As a student Doak fell under the influence of the Rev. Robert Smith, who had emigrated from Londonderry as a young boy, and for a while he taught at Smith's school in Pequea, Pennsylvania.

Soon after being ordained as a minister in 1777 Samuel Doak did missionary work in south west Virginia, but it was a call from the Hopewell and Concord congregations in the North Holston River settlement in Sullivan County, North Carolina (now East Tennessee) which settled his destiny. Samuel Doak was the first resident Presbyterian minister to witness in Tennessee and about 1778 he established the first church and first schoolhouse in the new world west of the Alleghenies.

President Theodore Roosevelt, in 'The Winning of the West', wrote of Doak: "Possessed of the vigorous energy that marks the true pioneer spirit, he determined to cast in his lot with the frontier folk. He walked through Maryland and Virginia, driving before him an old 'flea-bitten grey' horse, loaded with a sackful of books; crossed the Alleghenies, and came down along the blazed trails to the Holston settlements. The hardy people among whom he took up his abode were to appreciate his learning and religion as much as they admired his adventurous and indomitable temper; and the stern, hard, God-fearing man became a most powerful influence for good throughout the whole formative period of the South West".

The settlement Samuel Doak joined was of pioneering stock like himself and the two factors which united them was their faith, and survival from the harshness of the environment; hostile native Indian tribes and the advances of the British colonial forces.

Doak was by then married and on one occasion while he was absent from home obtaining provisions his wife Esther and baby miraculously escaped a Cherokee Indian attack. The barking of dogs alerted Esther Doak to the approach of Indians and with the baby asleep in her arms she slipped quietly into the woods. From her hiding place she anxiously watched the Indians enter the log cabin, carry out some of the furniture and set fire to the building. Remarkably the baby did not wake; for if it had and started to cry she and the child would have faced almost certain death from the Cherokees. When the Indians departed she went after dark, by a blind path, to the nearest frontier station, where she met up with her husband the next day.

Samuel Doak ministered for two years in Sullivan County at the Fork of Watauga and Holston Rivers. He moved to Washington County at the Little Limestone River in South Holston, near the spot where frontiersman Davy Crockett was born and grew up.

The threat of Indian attack was with the settlers daily, and, more than once, Samuel Doak's sermon was interrupted by a messenger bringing news of Cherokee savagery. On each occasion Doak would automatically pray to God for deliverance and abandon his meeting to join the other men in pursuit of the enemy. Doak's rifle was always at his side during services. Samuel Doak not only preached; he was the main teacher in the settlement and he founded not only dozens of churches in East Tennessee but schools as well.

SAMUEL DOAK AND THE PATRIOTS AT KINGS MOUNTAIN

A momentous hour came for Samuel Doak at Sycamore Shoals at Elizabethton in East Tennessee on September 25, 1780. There the Overmountain Men were mustering before the Battle of Kings Mountain and Colonel John Sevier asked the much respected pastor to speak to them. A vital stage had been reached in the Revolutionary War and the Wataugans, composed mainly of Scots-Irish families, were determined to breach the order of King George III of England that they were not to make further inroads on to the lands held by the Indians, west of the Allegheny Mountains.

The King's top soldier, Aberdonian Colonel Patrick Ferguson headed an army of Redcoats ready to crush the settlers, but there was a shock in store for them from the revolutionaries led by four redoubtable men: Virginians of an Ulster-Scots strain, Colonel Charles McDowell and Colonel William Campbell; Welshman Colonel Isaac Shelby and French Huguenot Colonel John Sevier.

On the morning of September 25 the men gathered with their families at Sycamore Shoals for a religious service, conducted by the Rev. Samuel Doak. The fiery sermon and prayer that Doak delivered that day steeled the Overmountain Men for the march up Gap Creek to the impending confrontation with the Redcoats, echoing the Old Testament battle cry - "The Sword of the Lord and Gideon".

Doak's words may have been characteristic of a cleric in the turbulent years of the late 18th century, but in the years since, they have struck a chord with millions of Americans who strongly cherish the liberty secured by the events at Kings Mountain.

SAMUEL DOAK'S SERMON AND PRAYER AT SYCAMORE SHOALS: SEPTEMBER 25, 1780

"My countrymen, you are about to set out on an expedition which is full of hardships and dangers, but one in which the Almighty will attend you. The Mother Country has her hands upon you, these American colonies, and takes that for which our fathers planted their homes in the wilderness - OUR LIBERTY. Taxation without representation and the quartering of soldiers in the homes of our people without their consent are evidence that the Crown of England would take from its American subjects the vast vestige of freedom. Your brethren across the mountains are crying like Macedonia unto your help. God forbid that you shall refuse to hear and answer their call - but the call of your brethren is not all. The enemy is marching hither to destroy your homes.

"Brave men, you are not unacquainted with battle. Your hands have already been taught to war and your fingers to fight. You have wrested these beautiful valleys of the Holston and Watauga from the savage hand. Will you tarry now until the other enemy carries fire and sword to your very doors? No, it shall not be. Go forth then in the strength of your manhood to the aid of your brethren, the defence of your liberty and the protection of your homes. And may the God of justice be with you and give you victory.

"Let us Pray.

"Almighty and gracious God! Thou hast been the refuge and strength of Thy people in all ages. In time of sorest need we have learned to come to Thee - our Rock and our Fortress. Thou knowest the dangers and snares that surround us on march and in battle. Thou knowest the dangers that constantly threaten the humble, but well beloved homes, which Thy servants have left behind them.

"O, in Thine infinite mercy, save us from the cruel hand of the savage, and of tyrant. Save the unprotected homes while fathers and husbands and sons are far away fighting for freedom and helping the oppressed. Thou, who promised to protect the sparrow in its flight, keep ceaseless watch, by day and by night, over our loved ones. The helpless woman and little children, we commit to Thy care. Thou wilt not leave them or forsake them in times of loneliness and anxiety and terror.

"O, God of Battle, arise in Thy might. Avenge the slaughter of Thy people. Confound those who plot for our destruction. Crown this mighty effort with victory, and smite those who exalt themselves against liberty and justice and truth. Help us as good soldiers to wield the SWORD OF THE LORD AND GIDEON".

"AMEN".

The British forces were routed by the Overmountain militia, Colonel Patrick Ferguson was killed and 225 of his men lay dead after a battle which lasted 65 minutes. For the victors their loss was small - 28 dead and 62 wounded, with the capture of 800 Redcoats and as much booty as they could lay their hands on. Kings Mountain was the turning point in the Revolutionary War and for the Scots-Irish militia men it was the sign to ignore the King and move on to new frontiers.

Samuel Doak, meanwhile, removed himself to the battlefield he knew best, winning souls for Christ and he was instrumental in opening new churches in other parts of East Tennessee, including Carter's Valley where Ulster-born settlers like Joseph Rogers and the Crocketts had set up home.

By 1785, Doak had organised Abingdon Presbytery under the Synod of Philadelphia and incorporating the churches of East Tennessee and south west Virginia. Within a decade this Presbytery extended to 36 congregations and a dozen ministers. Doak founded the Martin Academy and until the beginning of the 19th century it was the main seat of learning in this most westerly part of the frontier. It became Washington College in 1795.

The austere Calvinism Doak stood for left its mark on the community he served and it was said "his habits were those of the student, teacher and divine". One of the first graduates of Washington College was Doak's son John Whitefield Doak, who with his brother Samuel Witherspoon Doak became Presbyterian ministers. The Doaks had six children, two sons and four daughters in their marriage of 30-odd years, which ended with Esther Doak's death in 1807. In 1818, the same year that he resigned as president of Washington College, Samuel Doak married Margaret McEwen, a widow from Blount County.

On retirement from Washington College, at the age of 69, Doak moved to nearby Greeneville in East Tennessee to help his son Samuel Witherspoon with teaching duties at a classical school named Tusculum. He spent the last 12 years of his life there giving "a good and practical education" to up to 70 pupils.

For all his conservatism on theological matters, Samuel Doak was very strongly opposed to slavery, then actively pursued over a large part of the south west territory. His pulpit denunciation led to bitter conflict with some of the leading slave owners in the region and, after personally freeing many blacks, he managed to send them to Ohio to live. The seeds of his anti-slavery principles were implanted in the minds of many of his students and this influence significantly harnessed the move towards the abolition of slavery some years after his death.

Doak's death on December 12, 1830 brought the frontier faithful to a standstill and when his remains were buried in Salem Presbyterian churchyard a multitude from a wide area gathered to pay their last respects. This man of learning and religion probably did more for Christianity on the American frontier than any other living soul.

This Virginian of Co. Antrim stock was "the first apostle of Presbyterianism in Tennessee" . . . "the pioneer of education in Tennessee" - the missionary stalwart who "educated and sent into Tennessee and the adjoining states a very large proportion of the church ministry and other professions who moulded the character of the early population and founded their civil and religious institutions".

Samuel Doak, in the best Calvinist tradition, led his people through a wilderness and pointed them in the right direction, both spiritually and educationally. The light that he shone on the frontier was an inspiration to so many and not surprisingly his memory lives on.

Another Virginian-born cleric of note at the time and close associate of Samuel Doak was the Rev. Samuel Carrick, who ministered to the first wave of Scots-Irish settlers who had set up home on the fertile banks of the Holston and French Broad Rivers, now the Tennessee River which flows through Knoxville city.

Lebanon in the Fork was the serene setting for the worship of God in what was then a virtual wilderness. Surrounded by 11 tall cedar trees and in full view of the idyllic fork which links the winding Holston and French Broad Rivers, the Rev. Carrick used as his pulpit an old Indian mound for the first open-air service in 1791. And the text that he chose for his sermon that day was Second Corinthians chapter 5, verse 20 - "Now then, we are ambassadors for Christ as though God did beseech you by us; we pray you in God's stead, by ye reconciled to God".

Samuel Carrick, like the people he was ministering to at Lebanon in the Fork, was Scots-Irish. His parents were born in Ulster and had moved about the mid-18th century to York County, Virginia, where Samuel was born. Carrick eventually became the first minister of First Knoxville Presbyterian Church, whose founding elders were of Ulster stock - James White, John Adair and George McNutt.

(1) - 'Lexington: Religion and Marriage' records that the census of 1850 revealed that Augusta County had a population of 11,484 whites and 4,561 blacks. Among the white population, at least two-thirds were

of Scots-Irish descent, the highest percentage of this strain in the Shenandoah Valley. Most of the churchgoers were Presbyterian (reformed and unreformed) with Methodists running a poor second.

Meade's list of distinguished old Virginian families shows the following percentage proportion: English 43.5, Irish 16.5, Scots 15.4, Welsh 12.6, German 9.9, and French 2.1. The percentage proportions of 2,856 names from all over Virginia is given for comparison: English 40.6, Scots 27.3, German 9.1, Welsh 8.4, Irish 8.1, French 6.3 and others 0.2. As most of the Irish settlers bore Scottish names it can accurately be assumed that 25 to 30 per cent of the people were Scots-Irish.

Almost all of the Scots-Irish settlers who travelled to the Shenandoah Valley arrived in America via the ports of Philadelphia and New Castle (Delaware). Today, many in the political, economical and social leadership of the Shenandoah Valley are descended from the original Scots-Irish settlers. They have established a sense of Scots-Irish identity in regions like Augusta and Rockbridge Counties that is unrivalled anywhere in the United States, except perhaps in East Tennessee. These Americans exude great pride in their Scots-Irish roots, although a large number are totaly unaware of what part of Ulster their families originally left.

Carry me back *to old Virginny*

Carry me back to old Virginny,
There's where the cotton and corn and taters grow,
There's where the birds warble sweet in the spring time,
There's where the old darkey's heart am long'd to go.
There's where I laboured so hard for old Mas-sa,
Day after day in the field of yellow corn,
No place on earth do I love more sincerely
Than old Virginny, the state where I was born.

Chorus
Carry me back to old Virginny,
There's where the cotton and the corn and taters grow
There's where the birds warble sweet in the spring time,
There's where the old darkey's heart am long'd to go.

Carry me back to old Virginny, 'There let me live till I wither and decay,
Long by the old dis-mal swamp have I wandered,
There's where this old darkey's life will pass away.
Mas-sa and Mis-sis have long gone before me,
Soon we will meet on that bright and golden shore,
There we'll be happy and free from all sorrow,
There's where we'll meet and we'll never part no more.

Chorus

• Carry Me Back To Old Virginny (Virginia) is the state song of Virginia. It
was composed in 1875 by James Bland, a Negro songwriter and minstrel. It
was adopted as the state song in 1940

★★★

10

Virginians *at Kings Mountain*

Four hundred Virginians, mostly of Scots-Irish stock, played a significant role in winning the Battle of Kings Mountain in South Carolina on October 7, 1780 which proved to be the turning point in the American Revolutionary War.

At the head of the Virginian militia was Colonel William Campbell, who was born in Augusta County son of an Ulsterman, Charles Campbell, who was one of the earliest settlers in the region. After his father's death William Campbell moved in 1767, with his mother and four sisters, to the frontier of the Holston Valley, close to North Carolina territory which today extends into Tennessee.

He became a justice of the peace for Fincastle County in Virginia and as a soldier rose from captain to colonel in the Virginia militia just as the Revolutionary War was getting underway. After Kings Mountain he was elevated to brigadier general and commanded his regiment at the Siege of Yorktown. He was married to Elizabeth Henry, but died in 1781 aged only 36 - after just being elected state legislator.

Campbell, six foot in height, was the overall commander at Kings Mountain having been selected in consultations involving the other militia leaders from North Carolina and South Carolina - John Sevier, of a Huguenot family, Isaac Shelby of Welsh connections and Charles McDowell, like Campbell, from Scots-Irish roots. Colonel McDowell had distinguished himself as a Revolutionary leader in South Carolina and though senior to William Campbell in service he gave way to the young Virginian officer.

A feature of the Kings Mountain engagement was that all but one of the participants were American. There were patriot volunteers on the side of independence against loyalists who favoured the continuation of British rule in the colonies. The one notable exception was a Scot, Colonel Patrick Ferguson, an Aberdonian attached to His Majesty's 71st Highlanders. As the leading soldier in the British Army of the day, Ferguson was drafted in to lead a force of American loyalists to quell the rebellion and it was an action that was to tragically cost him his life.

The loyalists who backed the Crown at Kings Mountain came from a variety of backgrounds. Many were highland Scots, like Ferguson, and some were English settlers with strong Tory and Anglican roots. They came largely from North Carolina, and New York, the most loyalist of the American states during the Revolutionary War, but a state which paradoxically was the first to vote for independence.

Patrick Ferguson, the inventor of the first breechloading rifle used in the British Army, served under the command of Lord Cornwallis at Charleston and as Inspector of the Militia in the Southern Provinces he raised a loyalist militia force of some 4,000.

Both sides in the American dispute violently assailed one another, with attacks being carried out by both the loyalist factions and the revolutionary groups. Throughout the summer and autumn of 1780 these continued with ferocity.

It was the western region, across the Blue Ridge Mountains, which was causing Ferguson most worry and he sent a message to the Overmountain men to "desist from their opposition to the British arms, and take protection under his standard". If they did not Ferguson threatened to "march the loyalist army over the mountain, hang their leaders and lay their country waste with fire and sword".

The message had the opposite result: the Overmountain men began preparing for anything which Ferguson saw fit to throw at him, their resolve was to maintain their cultural identity and their independence.

The call to arms spread like wildfire among the mountain people and on September 25, on the flats at Sycamore Shoals, the territory that today encapsulates the town of Elizabethton close to Johnson City in North East Tennessee, a large gathering of settlers, in excess of 1,000 assembled.

Few of these combatants had the appearance of soldiers going into battle; they were small dirt farmers who had just left their lands, garbed in rough mountain-style clothes and carrying the barest of utensils. The most effective weapon each shouldered was the Kentucky long rifle, the traditional firepower of the American frontier. John Sevier commanded 240 men from Washington County (then North Carolina now Tennessee); Isaac Shelby a similar force from nearby Sullivan County; William Campbell led 400 Virginians and Charles McDowell 160 from South Carolina. More were to join from South Carolina.

The womenfolk also gathered at Sycamore Shoals to bid their farewells and to ensure that the volunteers had enough food and clothing for the assignment. And there was the Rev. Samuel Doak - his presence was significant in bringing spiritual guidance to those preparing for battle.

Doak, a Scots-Irish Presbyterian minister in the best traditions of the 18th century Calvinism, likened the cause of the Overmountain settlers to that of Gideon and his people in opposing the Midianites in Biblical times. "The Sword of the Lord and Gideon" he offered as the battle cry, with the assembled gathering loudly echoing his words before starting off on horseback on the long journey to face Ferguson and the loyalists.

It took 10 days before the patriot force came in sight of Ferguson's army: the distinctive red uniforms of the loyalists standing out in the rugged mountain terrain. Campbell's men dug into the wooded areas, while Ferguson decided on an open ridge for his base. After reviewing the platoons under his command, Campbell advised anyone who did not wish to fight to head for home immediately. There were no takers and after he ordered them to "shout like hell and fight like devils" his men responded to the first fire mounted from the Tory ranks.

The battle lasted 65 minutes, the revolutionary forces using Indian-style tactics to out-manoeuvre the loyalists from the back of every tree, rock and shrub. There was much hand-to-hand fighting and the prowess of the long riflemen gradually took its toll. The Redcoats were forced to defend their position with bayonets as the Overmountain men closed in. Colonel Ferguson, probably sensing defeat, had to personally ward off attacks from all sides. A rifle shot struck him in the head and slumping in the saddle he dropped from his horse, dead. His command was taken by Captain Abraham DePeyster, who had engaged the mountainmen in a previous battle at Musgrove's Mill.

It was a hopeless cause. The loyalists were encircled and in panic some waved white flags of surrender. But the shooting continued, with many of the patriots unaware of the significance of the white flags.

They were not professional soldiers and the revenge factor surfaced as previous atrocities committed by loyalists came to mind. Eventually, Colonel Campbell managed to bring about a ceasefire among his ranks by calling out: "For God's sake, don't shoot. It is murder to kill them now, for they have raised their flags". DePeyster protested at the behaviour of the patriots: "It's damned unfair, damned unfair". Campbell calmly ignored the protestations, calling on loyalists to sit down as "prisoners".

The Overmountain men had fairly minimal casualties compared to the loyalists: 28 killed and 62 wounded against 225 dead, 163 wounded and about 800 taken prisoner. Kings Mountain was the watershed in the Revolutionary War, the left flank of Lord Cornwallis had been effectively shattered and the British were never again able to muster a loyalist force of size from American society.

One of the Virginians who distinguished himself at Kings Mountain alongside William Campbell was Captain Gilbert Christian. He was the son and grandson of Ulster Presbyterians who left Co. Antrim in 1732, settling in Pennsylvania and then Virginia.

His grandfather Gilbert (born 1678) and his wife Elizabeth Margaret Richardson (born 1702 in Ireland) settled in Augusta County. Their son Robert, who was also born in Ireland, was recruiting officer for the Virginia militia in Augusta County during the Indian and Revolutionary Wars. The family had settled on Beverley Manor lands in Augusta about 1733 and there were two other sons John and William and a sister Mary. Most of their descendants went to Kentucky and Tennessee. Mary Christian first married John Moffett and when he died she wed James Trimble. A descendant was Allen Trimble, a Governor of Ohio.

Gilbert II won his captain's stripes while commanding the Sullivan County Militia and gained significant repute as an Indian fighter. After Kings Mountain he was promoted to major and eventually Colonel during expeditions to quell Indian unrest. He was a justice of the peace in Sullivan County and his son Robert married a daughter of John Adair, the Ballymena, Co. Antrim man, who is credited with raising the money to arm and equip the revolutionary force at Kings Mountain.

Among the Ulster-born soldiers in the Virginia line at Kings Mountain were Bellingsby Gibson (born near Londonderry in 1750 and a resident of Augusta County); James Laird (born Co. Antrim 1735 and a resident of Washington County); Captain Samuel Ware (born Co. Antrim 1750 and later to become involved in the convention which drew up the constitution of Tennessee) and Major William Candler (born Belfast 1736 and a resident of Augusta County).

Another Kings Mountain veteran was Brigadier General George Rutledge (born Co. Tyrone 1755), who lived for a time in Augusta County, Virginia. Most of the Virginia line at Kings Mountain were first or second generation Ulster-Scots.

George Rutledge succeeded John Sevier in the foremost Tennessee army position when Sevier became the state's first Governor in 1796. He represented Sullivan County in the first Tennessee legislature and was a senator in the third. The county seat of Grainger County, Tennessee is named in his honour. George Rutledge was married to Annie Armstrong, a member of a family who moved from Co. Fermanagh in the west of Ulster. William Rutledge, General George's father, set up home at Tinkling Spring in Augusta County, Virginia and there he married Eleanor Caldwell, who was born in Co. Cavan, Ireland. Other Rutledges who moved from Ulster were brothers Thomas and John and sisters Jane and Catherine.

The Rutledges were prominent members at the Tinkling Spring Presbyterian meeting house, but when land became available in North Carolina in 1777 they set off in hot pursuit. By 1783 they had acquired a land grant of 450 acres at the Holston River region, now Sullivan County in East Tennessee.

Decisive moment *in the Revolutionary War*

The critical student of American history never ceases to look with wonder and surprise at the Battle of Kings Mountain. It came like a thunderbolt from the skies, warning the British Crown, that subjugation of the Colonies was an impossibility. There is no event in the entire history of the American Revolution where the Providence of God is so manifest.

"How strange that this Scotch-Irish people, of such iron will and determined character, should have been gathered and secreted in the rich valleys beyond the Mountains, to be there trained by the hardships of Indian warfare, and held in reserve for the most critical moment in the American Revolution, when at their own suggestion they should come forth from their mountain fastnesses and strike a blow in favour of American freedom, which would make the ultimate and final success of this struggle inevitable. The Providence, that favours the right, moved upon the hearts of this people; they felt the hour for them to do their part had come; they went forth to battle, and the God of battles gave them the victory.

"There can be no question, but that the Battle of Kings Mountain was the turning point of the American Revolution; and these Scotch-Irish heroes, leaping like stalwart giants from their mountain home, did the wonderful work, and did it effectively. They little reckoned on the far-reaching consequence of what they had done.

"The people of this land will perhaps never fully realise the debt of gratitude they owe these fearless Scots-Irishmen, who, in the hour of their country's despair, rose in their might like a whirlwind of fire and swept to destruction the bright hopes of subjugation, which animated the British Crown." - part of an address delivered by the Rev. J.H. Bryson, of Huntsville, Alabama, before the Scotch-Irish Society of America at its annual meeting in Lexington, Virginia on June 20, 1895.

★★★

11

George Washington *and the Scots-Irish*

If defeated everywhere else I will make my stand for liberty among the Scots-Irish of my native Virginia" - the words of the first President of the United States General George Washington, who throughout the Revolutionary War expressed his high regard for the American troops of Ulster origin.

Washington was impressed by the Scots-Irish tenacity of spirit, the determination to see a thing right through to the end. From his days growing up in Virginia the founding father of America was comfortable in the company of the Scots-Irish settlers and, although of English background himself, he came to appreciate at close hand the sturdy characteristics of his Ulster neighbours on the frontier.

Henry Alexander Clark, who was born in Newry, Co. Down, had a close association with George Washington through growing up in Virginia and their involvement in the local militia. Clark had moved from the north of Ireland to America with his family in the early 18th century and his parents William Richard and Mary Elizabeth Rogers Clark were typical Presbyterian frontier settlers of the period.

According to family sources, Henry Alexander Clark "lived by his wits and his fists and survived" and he is recorded in 1749 as being a chain-carrier for a young George Washington, then a surveyor in Virginia. When Washington was made colonel of the Virginia Militia, Clark was his orderly sergeant and they made frequent trips across the Blue Ridge Mountains for surveying expeditions and to engage the French and the Indians.

The Clark family had been close neighbours of George Washington's parents Augustine and Mary, when they lived at Ferry Farm, Westmoreland County in eastern Virginia. Henry Alexander Clark married English-born Amelia Stafford and they had three sons William, Robert and James, all of whom served in the Revolutionary War under General Washington, in an undercover role.

In 1746, when George Washington was 14, he was apprenticed to survey the lands of Virginia and needing an assistant he recruited Henry Alexander Clark, who was a few years older and wise to the ways of frontier life. Together for several years they roamed the foothills of the Blue Ridge Mountains. Later, when a 20-year-old George Washington was given a commission as major in the Virginia Militia, he named Clark as his adjutant and they both saw action quickly.

About 1754, Washington received reports that French troops were coming from Canada into land west of the Allegheny Mountains, which today would be in the state of West Virginia. This was territory which the British and Virginians claimed, but it was still essentially Indian country. The French had begun to build forts on the land and to befriend the Indians, but Washington took the view that the French had no right to settle in this region as families from the Valley of Virginia had already built homes there.

Robert Dunwiddie, Governor of Virginia, ordered the French off the land and asked Washington to convey this in a letter to commanders at the new French fort. Winter weather was going to make the journey difficult and dangerous, but this was the kind of adventure Washington liked and the Governor knew he could be trusted with the job.

Washington invited Henry Alexander Clark to accompany him and they rode horseback over the Blue Ridge Mountains where more supplies were obtained for the trip. These included food, tents, and presents for friendly Indians. They were given pack horses to carry supplies and four men to assist and, on the way, they persuaded explorer and Indian trader Christopher Gist to act as their guide.

Washington and his group travelled 200 miles to deliver the letter to the French commander and waited several days for a reply. In conversation with French troops and Indians at the fort, it soon became clear to Washington and Clark that the French had no intention of moving off the lands.

The group headed back as soon as they received the negative reply from the French commander and such was the weather that it took them a month to make the Governor's base at Williamsburg. It was agreed Virginians would have to fortify their land west of the Allegheny Mountains and Washington and Clark were sent with a detachment of soldiers to erect the first fort on lands situated on present-day Pittsburgh, Pennsylvania. The fort was built of huge undressed logs from the surrounding forest and General Edward Braddock brought 1,000 soldiers from England to help defend it.

Washington was one of the American officers serving under Braddock and both he and Clark warned that fighting conventional English-style was disastrous along the frontier. The French, drilled by the Indians, fought from the gullies and behind trees and Braddock was among those killed.

Washington miraculously survived - it was reported two horses were shot from under him, three bullets went through his hat and one through his clothes, but he was uninjured. Clark got some shots in his clothing and a wound, but in leading the Virginia militia his tactics were to fight from behind trees. This helped turn the tide.

For their heroics in defending the frontier fort, George Washington was made commander of the Virginia forces and Henry Alexander Clark his chief aide. The French and Indian war ended with a peace treaty signed in 1763, but the irony was that 13 years later, Washington and Clark were to become heavily involved in the struggle for freedom by the 13 American colonies against the British Crown.

Washington's personal situation changed shortly after the French/Indian wars when his brother Lawrence died of ill-health and his baby daughter died the following year. George was left in charge of the estate after Lawrence's wife married again, surrendering her claim to the estate. George inherited Mount Vernon and for help he again called upon his long-time Scots-Irish friend Henry Alexander Clark.

Clark, by this time, was ill from fatigue and exposure on the frontier and an old injury at Ford Braddock was causing him pain. He was unable to accompany Washington when he took up command of the Revolutionary Army and was assigned home duties. These included arranging supplies and provisions to be sent to the front for Washington's army and helping to organise undercover units. He was also guardian of Mrs. Washington and the Mount Vernon estate.

The Army Intelligence Service was one of his duties, because the tactics and strategy of frontier warfare depended as much on gathering information behind enemy lines as on soldiers and weapons. Henry Alexander Clark was a master of disguise in this situation and his contribution to the war effort was highly significant.

Clark's three sons, William, Robert and James were also recruited to the secret service for the duration of the war, but they were never listed in any army records, for security reasons. They posed as country yokels, in appearance, action, and speech; acted dumb and ignorant, but in reality they were fully alert to what was going on around them.

The three were assigned to the Northern colonies for service and were joined by another young man of Scots-Irish extraction Robert McClellan, whose descendant George Brinton McClellan was a general in the Union Army during the American Civil War. The four, all accurate marksmen, rehearsed their yokel acts in the deep woods and then practised it on the frontier settlers before moving into the war zone against the British. Working underground, they were of great value to the war effort.

For his outstanding services in the Revolutionary War, Henry Alexander Clark was awarded a land grant in Tennessee, but he was too old to make the journey by covered wagon from Virginia and he sent his three sons instead to settle in Pickett County on the Cumberland Mountain plateau. A settlement was created in an area today known as Clark Mountain and out of a wilderness the family helped found a Presbyterian church and a school, as was the tradition on the frontier at the time.

12

Sam Houston's roots *in Virginia*

Sam Houston may have made his name in Tennessee and Texas, but he was a Virginian of second generation Scots-Irish stock from the Larne area in Co. Antrim. Sam, who always liked to be known as Samuel, was born in Timber Ridge, Rockbridge County, Virginia on March 2, 1793, about seven miles from Lexington.

His grandfather John Huston (the name was changed to Houston when they arrived in America) emigrated from Ulster about 1740 and with other Presbyterian kinsfolk from Co. Antrim he settled in the Valley of Virginia after landing in Pennsylvania.

John Houston was the principal founder of the Providence Presbyterian Church at Rockbridge County in 1746, where the preacher was the Rev. John Brown, who emigrated from Londonderry. John Houston was the congregation's first elder and with his brother Samuel often held prayer meetings at their homes. Sam Houston's father, Major Sam Houston, was a veteran of the Revolutionary War who continued soldiering into the 19th century. He died in 1807 while on a tour inspection of frontier army posts and this prompted the family to move to Tennessee.

The Houston family tree contains a long line of Presbyterian ministers and elders. Major James Houston, a nephew of John Houston, was an elder of Maryville Presbyterian in East Tennessee and six of his daughters married church ministers. Another pastor in the family was the Rev. Samuel Houston, a cousin of Sam, and his son the Rev. Samuel Rutherford Houston was a missionary to Greece. The Rev. Samuel Doak, who ministered to the Overmountain Men before they engaged in the Battle of Kings Mountain in 1780, was also of the Houston clan.

Sam's mother, Elizabeth Paxton Houston, was a devout Presbyterian who according to records of the time was "gifted with intellectual and moral qualities" above that of most women in the frontier. It was said her life was characterised by "purity and benevolence". When her husband died in 1807 she moved with her nine children - six sons and three daughters - from Virginia in the covered wagons to Maryville, Blount County in Tennessee. There she joined the Baker's Creek Presbyterian Church and twice and often three times a week she and the children walked the four miles over the hills to worship.

It was in this environment that Sam Houston grew up, his mother's Christian counselling an obvious influence on him. Later Sam admitted that the early impressions passed on from his mother far outlived all the wisdom of later life.

Sam Houston left a detailed description of life among the early immigrants in the Shenandoah Valley. "Their cabins had but one door and no windows except holes between the logs and the light shone down from the top of a log chimney. Their bedsteads . . . . mostly crosssticks with thick clapboards on which were laid skins of bears and buffaloes. Their food consisted chiefly of venison, bear meat, buffalo, raccoon, turkey, pheasant, wild geese and pigeons, the river fish and eels, Irish potatoes, pumpkins, turnips and cabbages. Their bread was coarse Indian corn meal made in wooden morters by wooden pestles. Some had pewter basins, plates and tankards, but most persons used trenchers and platters made . . . . out of yellow poplar wood."

Houston remembers with affection his father's "squared log house with its glass windows, which was the admiration and wonder of the neighbours".

After a career as a teacher and militiaman Sam Houston moved into politics and he was elected to the United States Congress in 1823, and re-elected in 1825. Andrew Jackson was Houston's political mentor and it is recorded that in his four years in Congress, Sam displayed "remarkable qualities of statesmanship". Sam was elected Governor of Tennessee in 1827, and was re-elected in 1829.

In 1833 Sam moved to Texas, where a revolution was being planned to overthrow Mexican rule. He was welcomed by the American colonists at Nacogdoches and took part in talks with Comanche Indian chiefs on disputed boundary questions in the San Antonio region. The welfare of the native Americans remained Sam's main concern.

Houston was in the vanguard of the independence movement and he sat on the convention at San Felipe de Austin which set in train the breakaway from Mexico. He was sworn in as major-general and commander-in-chief of the new revolutionary army, but time was not on his side - Mexican President Santa Anna was closing in with 5,000 men in three columns.

The Mexicans reached San Antonio and laid siege on The Alamo, an old walled Franciscan mission where 185 Texans and a collection of women, children and black slaves were holed up. Defending the fort were two old associates of Houston - Tennessean frontiersman Davy Crockett and Colonel Jim Bowie, but the situation was impossible and before reinforcements could be sent all able-bodied men at the station were killed.

The Alamo stirred Houston for action and he managed to recruit enough men - just over 700 - in the Texas auxiliaries to confront Santa Anna at the Battle of San Jacinto. The Texans were heavily outnumbered - there were 1,800 Mexicans, but in 20 minutes Houston's men, charging to the cry "Remember The Alamo", were victorious. The Mexicans lost 630 killed and had 730 taken prisoner, among them Santa Anna, and within a short time the Mexican President had given his consent to independence for Texas. Houston, injured in the ankle in the battle, became the new republic's first president.

Houston retired as President of Texas in 1844 and in March, 1846 he was elected as Senator to Washington from the Lone Star state. Texas had been admitted as a state of the Union on December 29, 1845 and Houston served for 14 years as a senator. During his senatorship he opposed the Southern doctrine that Congress had no right to legislate on slavery in the territories and he advocated California as a state of the Union and the development of the Pacific railroad through Texas.

In 1859 Sam was elected Governor of Texas as an Independent and served until March, 1861, when, on the enrolment of the state as a member of the Confederacy, he refused to take the necessary official oath and recognise the authority of the new convention. He was forced out of office by the Confederate politicians. By now an old man, Houston was war-weary and did not resist. He wanted no more blood spilt among his own people. Sam retired to his farm at Huntsville and after an illness of five weeks he died on July 26, 1863, aged 70, as the Civil War was in progress.

A few days before Sam died he made his will, and, in the fifth clause, he said: "To my eldest son, Sam Houston, I bequeath my sword, worn in the battle of San Jacinto, to be drawn only in defense of the constitution, and laws, and liberties of his country. If any attempt be made to assail one of these, I wish it to be used in its vindication".

The Civil War had already begun and Sam Jun., then only 20, was a Confederate soldier and, much to Sam Houston's regret, the American states were at each other's throats.

It was American President John F. Kennedy, who said of Sam Houston: "He was one of the most independent, unique, popular, forceful and dramatic individuals ever to enter the Senate Chamber. He was in turn magnanimous, vindictive, affectionate yet cruel, eccentric yet self-conscious, faithful yet opportunistic. But Sam Houston's contradictions actually confirm his one basic consistent quality: indomitable individualism, sometimes spectacular, sometimes crude, sometimes mysterious, but always courageous".

Sam's courage was undoubtedly fired by the unique Scots-Irish characteristic that tamed the frontier.

13

First Scots-Irish *church settlements in the Shenandoah*

C o. Antrim-born John Craig was the first Presbyterian cleric to minister full-time in the Shenandoah Valley and his orthodox but far-seeing Calvinistic teachings left an indelible mark on the people of the region in the 250 years since.

The Rev. Craig's parents had been born in Scotland and moved to Dunagore (Dunager) parish in the north of Ireland during the Scottish plantation settlements of Ulster in the 17th century. The Craigs were a pious, God-fearing couple who were determined to give their son, who was born in 1709, a sound education. At an early age, John was sent to the University of Edinburgh, where, in 1733, he graduated with a Master of Arts degree.

John Craig decided that he had a mission for Christ on the American frontier and, soon after arrival at New Castle in Delaware, as a 25-year-old, he began theological studies under the tuition of the Rev. John Thomson, of Chestnut Level in Pennsylvania. In 1737, he was invited by the Donegal Presbytery in Pennsylvania to become a licensed preacher and by 1740 he was fully qualified to face the considerable challenge of witnessing in the Shenandoah Valley, which was then rapidly becoming the magnet for many Scots-Irish settlers in from Pennsylvania.

Craig spent the winter of 1739-40 as an itinerant preacher in Virginia and it prepared him for the ministerial charge that was to come. It was to Tinkling Spring, on the southern part of the Beverley Manor lands in the Shenandoah, that John Craig was sent after a call to the Donegal

Presbytery and among the first to greet him was Donegal (Ireland)-born John Lewis, who had pioneered this tract of land a decade earlier.

In addition to the Lewises, other Scots-Irish families who worshipped at Tinkling Spring were the Campbells, Christians, Kerrs, Finleys, Prestons, Stuarts, Bells, Alexanders, Thompsons and Pattons.

The Rev. James Anderson, from the Donegal Presbytery, had made occasional journeys into the Valley of Virginia to establish some form of church organisation and the first Tinkling Spring meeting house was set up in 1737. In November, 1738, Anderson preached in the Staunton home of John Lewis, which was one of the largest buildings in the settlement, and neighbours gathered for the unique occasion - the first religious sermon to be preached in the Shenandoah Valley. Then, only 11 families had procured titles for lands from landowner William Beverley, but by 1740 when John Craig arrived this had increased to 37.

The "Triple Forks of the Shenandoah" congregation (it also came under the name of the "Christian Society"), that called and settled the Rev. John Craig had two meeting houses - one at Tinkling Spring and the other, 11 miles north, at what became known as the "Stone Meeting House of Augusta".

James Anderson died in July, 1740, probably worn out by his arduous ministry on the frontier, and John Craig was ordained and installed by the Donegal Presbytery two months later. Craig was clearly a genuine witness to his Lord and a diligent teacher of the Biblical truths. He was a strong advocate of religious liberty and civic freedom and his teachings in this direction later inspired his successors to have them written into Virginian law. The Scots-Irish, like the Germans who settled the Valley of Virginia in the 18th century, believed that only an educated people could be a free people and in the absence of public schools, the home, church and community, they assumed responsibility for education.

John Craig was said to be "a man from God to a particular people at a particular time". His epitaph reads: "John Craig was a strong-minded and persevering minister, strictly orthodox and yet pungent in the application of the truth to the conscience".

Craig's only written sermon that has survived to the present-day is a 7,500 word discourse he delivered at Tinkling Spring in December, 1767, at the end of his 27-year ministry there. The sermon, divided into 55 divisions and sub-divisions, was based on a text taken from Second Samuel, chapter 23, verse five: "Yet He hath made with me an everlasting covenant, ordered in all things, and sure, for this is all my salvation, and all my desire". The sermon was dedicated by Craig to what he referred to as "my dear children".

Little detail is known about John Craig's wife, but he was married at Pennsylvania on June 11, 1744 and had a family. Daughters Mary and Patience married members of the Tinkling Spring congregation and with their husbands are buried in the old cemetery. Son George also remained in the congregation with his family.

During the latter part of his Tinkling Spring ministry, John Craig wrote: "From ye dream I had before I left Ireland when I came to ye settlement, I knew it to be the plot in Christ's vineyard where I was to labor."

The Tinkling Spring worshippers were strict Sabbatarians. All church business - by session, commissioners and congregation - was transacted on week-days. They walked or rode horseback to the meeting house on Sunday mornings, John Craig walked regularly to the church from his 335-acre Lewis Creek farm (close to present-day Staunton), a distance of about six miles as the crow flies. Some of the congregation carried long rifles as a precaution against Indian attack and the worship was a marathon affair, lasting for most of the day. The morning service began at 10 o'clock and went into recess at noon for a lunch period. The afternoon service lasted from one o'clock until sunset.

The Psalms were the cornerstone of the worship, taken from the Scottish Psalter, which included all 150 Psalms. The sacraments of the church were a vital part of the worship and it was estimated that the Rev. Craig baptised about 100 persons per year in the first decade of his ministry. The baptism was mostly of infants, although the occasional adult was listed. For the adult church member, the Communion of the Last Supper was the primary sacrament in the services.

These baptisms were scattered over a wide area of Virginia, from Jackson River in the Alleghenies on the west to Rockfish Valley east of the Blue Ridge Mountains and from Great Lick, now the town of Roanoke, to the Fairfax Line, just south of New Market, on the north - a vast area of some 10,000 square miles.

Lack of settled ministers in the region placed on John Craig a gruelling schedule of preaching duties throughout his Tinkling Spring ministry. During the period 1740-47 he was the only settled Presbyterian cleric in the entire colony of Virginia and he listed 36 locations where he   conferred the sacrament of baptism, 14 of them in private houses.

Outside of Tinkling Spring and Augusta Stone Churches, there were at least 10 Presbyterian settlements in the region seeking congregational status and their own pastors: North Mountain, South Mountain, Roanoke, James Rivers, Borden's Tract and Cook's Creek in Shenandoah Valley, and Rockfish Valley, Ivy Creek, Buck Mountain, and Woods Gap across the Blue Ridge Mountains to the east.

That John Craig successfully managed to bring the gospel to these scattered communities at a time when the means of transport was so limited is indeed remarkable. His spiritual capacity was almost inexhaustible and as a result of his personal testimony and witness the Shenandoah region is today dotted with Presbyterian churches. Craig, it is said, prepared the seed-bed for permanent Presbyterianism in Virginia, from which the church expanded west and south into states like Tennessee, Kentucky, North Carolina and Georgia.

• By 1763, Virginia had an estimated 16 Presbyterian ministers, six of whom were working in the Lexington Presbytery around the Shenandoah. At that time one-third of the southern population of America was in Virginia. In the Shenandoah region, there were an estimated 20,000 whites (mostly of Scots-Irish and German origin) and 1,000 black slaves.

SAMUEL BLACK - THE PIONEER PREACHER

Black is a very common surname in Northern Ireland and Scotland today, and indeed in the Valley of Virginia where many of this Presbyterian clan came and settled. Pioneer preacher, the Rev. Samuel Black, who ministered in Pennsylvania and Virginia, was the son of a Co. Down wool merchant, James Black, and probably the most illustrious of the family who emigrated in the 18th century.

Samuel Black, educated for the Presbyterian ministry in Edinburgh and licensed by the Armagh Presbytery in Ulster, landed at New Castle, Delaware in 1734 with his brothers John and Anthony. Samuel was authorised to preach by the Presbytery of Donegal in Pennsylvania in 1736 and became the minister of a new church at Brandywine in Chester County. However, his charge over a five-year period was not without controversy. The congregation divided on theological and moral grounds between the "old side" and the "new side" and charges against the Rev. Black of "drunkenness", "sowing dissension among his flock" and "a neglect of ministerial duties" were presented to the Presbytery in November 1740.

Renewed charges were made in the following May and he was suspended, pending an examination. The Synod, the highest court of the Presbyterian Church in America, met at Philadelphia to consider the matter, but there was a further split and it was another month before the charges could be heard against Mr. Black. After a protracted hearing he was found not guilty of all three charges, but the damage had been done and only a few worshippers rallied to his ministry. The pastoral relationship was dissolved.

Samuel Black accepted a call from the congregation of Conewago Church in Dauphin County, Pennsylvania and remained there until 1747. During this period, he had made occasional preaching visits to Virginia and a call eventually came from Rockfish and Mountain Plain congregation. This was the territory where the Rev. John Craig had been overseeing and the Rockfish Church had only been formed a year earlier.

Black was the first Presbyterian minister to settle in Albemarle County, Virginia, and both he and his son William taught at an adjoining school. He purchased 400 acres of land at Stockton's Creek and called his plantation home "Quantity and Quality". He was buried there in 1770, the only marker being an unlettered stone. This pioneer preacher had a turbulent ministry in Pennsylvania, but in Virginia his Christian witness and work was productive and with much blessing.

In "Sketches of Virginia, Historical and Biographical", W. H. Foote states of Black: "In every respect, his situation (Rockfish, Virginia) was well chosen; the people were enterprising, the soil good, the climate favourable, and the community a church-going people by habit. An amiable man of a retiring disposition, as infirmities came upon him he secluded himself more and more from the public labours of the ministry. He was orthodox in doctrine, and correct in his views of religious action and Christian principles, as has been evidenced by the fact that a goodly number of pious people were found at Rockfish; and his successors in the ministry saw evidence that God had blessed the ministry of His word by him. No production of his pen remains; and no great act marked the even tenor of his way. His influence, like that of multitudes, will be known in its wider or narrower diffusion, at the great day."

Samuel Black married Catherine Shaw in Pennsylvania during his Brandywine ministry and they had four sons and three daughters. Samuel's two brothers settled in Augusta County after a short spell in Pennsylvania. Members of the family fought in the Revolutionary War and on the Confederacy side during the Civil War.

14

Pioneering worship *at Timber Ridge*

The Timber Ridge Presbyterian Church in Rockbridge County, Virginia was founded by Scots-Irish families who moved into this part of the Shenandoah Valley during the 1730s. This is the oldest community in Rockbridge County (main town Lexington) and the church was the earliest in the area.

It was Ulsterman Ephriam McDowell who led his family and friends in 1737 on to the border lands they were to call Timber Ridge and, being strong Presbyterians, they continued to worship in the traditional manner they had been taught back in their former homeland.

McDowell and his compatriots set about erecting log cabin homes, but it was not until 1746 that they had a proper church meeting house - services, until then, were held in the various homes.

Worshippers of Timber Ridge and the adjoining New Providence congregation were "put into church order" during a missionary visit by the Rev. John Blair, from the Presbytery of Donegal in Pennsylvania, and the first minister, the Rev. William Dean, was called in 1748. He died before assuming his charge and it was not until 1755 that a replacement arrived - the Rev. John Brown, another of Ulster extraction.

At this time, the settlers were under constant threat of Indian attacks and one of John Brown's first duties as pastor of Timber Ridge was to organise a day of fasting and prayer on account of "the ongoing French/Indian Wars and the many murders committed by the Indians in the region."

The call to the Rev. John Brown was signed by 116 persons, with the first signature that of Co. Antrim man, John Houston, the grandfather of General Sam Houston, the Governor of Tennessee and Texas. Sam was born a few yards from the Timber Ridge Church. The list of signatures included the McDowells, Lyles, Davidsons, McClungs, Campbells, Paxtons, Thomsons, Mackeys and Alexanders - all families who had moved a few years earlier to America from the north of Ireland.

A stone church was erected in 1755/56, with John Lyle and James McClung heading the building committee. A marble tablet, bearing the date 1756, was erected on the front wall of the simple limestone structure, which sat on an acre of land deeded by Robert Houston.

The families donated generously to buy the building materials, but the work was carried out by voluntary labour, with the bare hands of the most able-bodied members. The sand used for "lyme" in the construction was carried by the women on horseback from South River, a distance of five miles. The women rode under protection of the men, who walked with long rifles at the ready through forests inhabited by Indian tribes.

The building of stone and lyme is the nave of the present Church. Daniel Lyle was the stonemason and his building has been in use as a church for 240 years, and is one of two such colonial structures west of the Blue Ridge, the other being Augusta Old Stone Presbyterian Church. The structure was designed as a fortress during the period of the French and Indian War. Some of Kerr's Creek settlers were saved from the massacre there because they were attending services at Timber Ridge.

The Timber Ridge Church of 1756 was described by local historians as "forty-four feet long, thirty-four feet wide, and fifteen feet high to the square, and the gebals built to the collar beams, with three doors. Two large doors, in the end of the house, and a little door, by the pulpit, nine windows, four on each side and one in the gebal end above. Also a little door on the other end ag't the window." Near the top of the south wall was the letters "I.B." for John Brown. When that wall was removed in 1900 for adding the wings, the stone was placed in the wall of the vestibule. The stone church had earthen floors with split logs for seats. The pulpit was at the north-western corner of the church. Each family had their own log, a tradition which was continued through the benches and pews, and even exists to some extent today.

Dr. James G. Leyburn, in his book *The Scotch-Irish*, tells about the all-day service, with two sermons about twelve points, compared with today's three point sermon. "The people would stand up and stretch when they needed to. During lunch, couples would court (talk with each other), under the watchful eye of their parents and other members of the congregation. Fathers would talk crops and weather, or perhaps politics. Mothers would compare stories of children or news of those who had moved westward. The church provided the opportunity to socialise."

Rev. J. A. Trostle wrote in his 1901 "Historical Sketch" that Timber Ridge was a long wooded hill. "This ridge extends from near North River (now the Maury), a short distance below Lexington, to a point within what is now Augusta County; the southern part of which was particularly known as Timber Ridge because of the amount of trees found on its sides and summit by these settlers, the rest of the valley being covered mostly with tall, coarse grass."

These settlers were strong in their belief in God, and in the need for both church and schools. They were persistent, some say stubborn, in character, and very frugal. Shenandoah historian Dr. Lyle Kinnear said: "They kept the Sabbath, and everything else they could get their hands on." They had defended their homes in Ireland, so they were trained for the frontier. They often came in clusters: from being relatives and neighbours in the North of Ireland to being relatives and neighbours in Augusta and Rockbridge Counties.

In the history of Rockbridge County many of these old families were outstanding. John Mackey came to the county around 1725 to hunt bear and deer, and other wild game. In time he built his home on Timber Ridge and brought his family to the "wilds of Virginia". His home was on land deeded to him many years later, and a descendant of his still owns this land. John was one of the first elders of Timber Ridge Presbyterian Church. He died in 1773, and is buried in the churchyard beside the stone church. The inscription on the stone which covers his grave reads:

"HERE LYES THE INT-RD BODY OF JOHN MCKY WHO DEPARTED THIS LIFE IN THE YEAR OF OUR LORD 1773 BEING THE 70 YEAR OF HIS AGE, AFTER LIVING A CHRIST-EN LIFE A LOVING HUSBAND A TENDER PARENT & A FAITHFUL FRIEND &C."

On the headstone is the date 1774. At the bottom of the flat stone is the inscription, "Remamber man As you pas by As you Are Now so once was i As J Am Now you soon Will be Therefore Think on Eternity."

• The spelling, capitalisation and punctuation in both quotations are as they were written on the stone.

The Presbyterians of Timber Ridge were not always a united people and doctrinal differences led to splits between those who adhered to the more evangelical 'New Lights' movement and the more traditional and formal 'Old Lights'. In the 19th century there were three different Presbyterian factions operating at Timber Ridge. One faction was the Seceders, who later became attached to the Associate Reformed Presbyterian Church. They confined themselves strictly to the singing of the metrical translations of the Psalms of David, a tradition that dates back to the Covenanters on the hillsides of Scotland.

A grammar school had been founded in 1749 by Robert Alexander, one of the Timber Ridge congregation, and this was eventually to become the Washington and Lee University at Lexington. It was the Timber Ridge congregation which generously funded the Liberty Hall school, and maintained it during the difficult years of the Revolutionary War of 1776-81. Washington and Lee is the oldest American institution of learning off the Atlantic seaboard and the fifth oldest university in the United States. In 1798 President George Washington granted the University the largest grant up to that time in the history of American education - 50,000 dollars.

It was written of the Timber Ridge settlers: "These liberty-loving, God-fearing people have ever stood for what was highest and best in the civil, intellectual and religious life of their chosen country, and many of them sealed with their life blood, their devotion to duty in times of trouble and warfare. Many of them bore arms during the early struggle for liberty, and in the Civil War, strife between the States there was scarcely a man left within the bounds of the congregation, and some of them never returned. During the early years of the settlement a large number of them fell victims to the treachery and cruelty of the Indians and their more savage and inhuman allies. Still, with their courage and fearlessness when the bugle of duty calls them to the camp and the battlefield, they were among the most peaceful and law-abiding citizens in the nation. Timber Ridge Church has had some of the most highly cultured

and deeply devout men who have ever lived in Virginia among her ministers in the years that have passed."

Many distinguished political figures, churchmen, educationalists and
captains of industry and business in Virginia and neighbouring states
have emanated from the families of the original Timber Ridge congregation. Sam Houston was probably the most illustrious, and Dr. Ephriam
McDowell, a grandson of the original settler of the same name, because
one of the most eminent surgeons in America in the early 19th century.
In 1812, he operated on James K. Polk, who was later to become United
States President. Polk, then only 17, was operated for the disease "Visicap
Calculus" and his health was restored after Dr. McDowell removed a
stone from his bladder, a highly delicate task at a time when medical
knowledge was not so advanced.

British Kings *who lost the American Colonies*

• George I (reigned 1714-1727). This German-born King hated and spoke little English.

• George II (reigned 1727-1760). Son of George I, he spoke English with a very pronounced German accent.

• George III (reigned 1760-1820). The grandson of George II, he was monarch during the Revolutionary War and conceded Crown rule in American. In the later years of his reign he went mad.

★★★

15

The Scots-Irish *and the Civil War*

T he Civil war of 1861-65 tragically split the American nation and in bloody encounters from North to South many lives were lost before the federal Union forces triumphed. Descendants of the Scots-Irish settlers who had pioneered the American frontier 100 years earlier distinguished themselves in the uniforms of both the Confederate and the Union Armies. The heroics of leading generals, middle ranking officers and ordinary privates are today part of American folklore. The soldiers, of Ulster lineage, listed in this book, were of the highest valour, fighting for a cause they believed in.

GENERAL THOMAS JONATHAN "STONEWALL" JACKSON

Civil War hero Thomas Jonathan Jackson, a Shenandoah man immortalised in the southern states of America as "Stonewall", was the great grandson of an Ulsterman who emigrated in 1748. "Stonewall" became renowned for his courage and military prowess during the bloody conflict between the states in the early 1860s and in a very short time he rose from being a major in the Confederate Army to become Major General, second only to General Robert E. Lee.

It was at the Battle of Bull Run in Virginia in July, 1861 that Jackson was given his nickname for it was said of him: "This is Jackson, standing a stone wall". The role he played in this battle brought "Stonewall" promotion to Major General.

Thomas Jonathan Jackson was made of stern stuff, following in the line of a doughty forebear John Jackson, who was born in the North of Ireland in 1715 and as "a respectable and prosperous tradesman" made the arduous voyage across the Atlantic to start a new life on the American frontier.

John Jackson's family were lowland Presbyterian Scots, who settled in Ulster during the 17th century Scottish Plantation and took part in the Siege of Londonderry of 1688-89 on behalf of Williamite Protestant cause The Jackson family were scattered across the north of Ireland; some were located in the north west of the Province around Londonderry/Coleraine, but others lived in Counties Antrim, Down and Armagh. The Birches area in Co. Armagh is said to be an area where members of "Stonewall" Jackson's family lived.

Various claims are made about exactly where in Ulster John Jackson, Thomas Jonathan Jackson's great grandfather, was born. In the biography of "Stonewall" Jackson by English writer Lieutenant Colonel G. F. R. Henderson a letter is referred to which attests that the ancestors of the great Confederate General had lived in the parish of Londonderry. This letter, Henderson states, was in the posession of Thomas Jackson Arnold, of Beverly, West Virginia, a nephew of General Jackson. Another report, of American origin, gives John Jackson's birthplace as near Coleraine in Co. Londonderry.

In the Birches/Tartaraghan area of Co. Armagh close to the shores of Lough Neagh, however, the local Jacksons are totally convinced that John Jackson was one of their kin. In fact, on July 22, 1967 a plaque was unveiled at a spot in Ballinary, a section of the Birches district, by the then United States Consul general for Northern Ireland. The plaque confirmed that this was the reputed site of the birthplace of John Jackson, great grandfather of Confederate General, Thomas Jonathan "Stonewall" Jackson (1824-1863). The Ballinary site is some 70 miles from Londonderry/Coleraine.

There are reportedly more Jacksons in the Birches/Tartaraghan region than in any other part of Ulster and today residents are totally convinced of their connection with the famous General's family. John Jackson, the original pioneer, is traced by the Co. Armagh Jacksons to be a grandson of a Robert Jackson and a son of John Jackson, who is buried in Tartaraghan Parish Churchyard.

Another John Jackson, from this area, fought with King William III at the Battle of the Boyne in 1690 and his sword and cutlass used in the battle have been displayed at Carrickfergus Castle in Co. Antrim. The Jacksons of Co. Armagh have always been strong supporters of the Orange cause in Ireland and today that tradition is manifested in their membership of the various Orange lodges in a region, where the Orange Order was founded in 1795. These Jacksons primarily belong to the Church of Ireland (Episcopal) and if the American link is true, it would have meant that John Jackson and his family almost certainly converted to Presbyterianism when they reached America.

John Jackson reached Maryland in 1748 after a brief sojourn in London where he very probably met the woman he was to marry in America. Elizabeth Cummins was the daughter of a London hotelier, who, when her father died and her mother remarried, decided to move to America. She was a well-educated woman, of a large stature, and "as remarkable for her strength of intellect as for beauty and physical vigour."

Elizabeth married John Jackson in 1755 and within two years they headed to the Valley of Virginia with the great flow of Scot-Irish families. They made a home at Moorefield in Hardy County, West Virginia, but after the French/ Indian wars of the 1750s/1760s they trekked 150 miles westwards to find new bearings at Buckhannon in Randolph County, Virginia.

John Jackson was "a spare diminutive man, of quiet, but determined character, sound judgment and excellent morals." In his exploits as an Indian fighter he amassed sizeable land holdings in the Shenandoah region and these he distributed to his eight children. The Jacksons became one of the leading families in the Valley, in terms of wealth and influence.

Governor Harry Lee appointed John an Indian scout in Western Virginia, he was a Randolph County justice and in 1789, at the age of 74, he served as captain of a frontier militia company. Elizabeth, who had possession of 3,000 acres of land in her own right at Buckhannon, died in 1828, at the age of 105. In her earlier years on the Virginian frontier, Elizabeth Jackson displayed great courage in thwarting Indian attacks on the family homestead and even in the most dangerous situations, she never wilted.

Two of John and Elizabeth's sons rose to high office. Edward (1759-1828), the grandfather of "Stonewall", was Randolph County surveyor, colonel of militia, commissioner of revenue and high sheriff. He represented Lewis County in the Virginia Assembly and was a citizen who "acquired some knowledge of medicine, was an expert millwright, and a farmer of more than usual ability."

George Jackson, his older brother, was elected to the American Congress for three terms and was a close associate of General Andrew Jackson, another of Scots-Irish vintage who rose to the Presidency in 1828. George had served with distinction in the Revolutionary War, reaching the rank of colonel. George Jackson and Andrew Jackson were not related, but they did talk frequently about their first generation Ulster connections who had moved to America several decades earlier. George Jackson's son John George Jackson, replaced his father in Congress and, as a lawyer, he was an articulate spokesman in Washington for the Shenandoah dwellers.

Jonathan Jackson, father of "Stonewall", studied law at the Clarksburg office of his uncle and although he married the daughter of a merchant from Parlsbury, West Virginia, Julia Beeleith Neale, he was never a man of great wealth. He died when "Stonewall" was only three.

John George Jackson married Mary Payne, of Philadelphia, a sister of Dolly Madison, wife of James Madison, the fourth President of the United States. This added to the weight of Jackson influence at the highest level and John George was appointed by Madison's successor in the White House, James Monroe, as the first federal judge for the Western region of Virginia. A brother of John George, Edward Brake Jackson was an army surgeon during the Creek Indian war of 1812, a Clarksburg doctor, and a member of the American Congress for four years.

Thomas Jonathan Jackson inherited a noble tradition of soldiering and public service and it was appropriate that he should be given a Congressional appointment to the top American military academy at West Point in 1842.

"Stonewall" had a tough upbringing, his father had left little property on his death and his mother was forced to seek the help of her relatives and the Free Masons to rear the three children - two sons Tom ("Stonewall") and Warren and a daughter Laura. Four years after her husband's death, Julia Beeleith Neale Jackson died - tragically, Thomas Jonathan was an orphan at seven and with his brother and sister, he went to live with his father's half brother on a Western Virginia farm.

"Stonewall" was a youth of "exemplary habits, of indomitable will and undoubted courage", but the Virginia frontier of the early 19th century was a tough breeding ground for even one with his integrity and doggedness to succeed in life. His uncle was a kind guardian, but with unscrupulous and violent traits. The year before "Stonewall" received the West Point call he became a constable of the county, with duties to execute court decrees, serve warrants, summon witnesses and collect debts. He was only 17 at the time, but on the threshold of a distinguished military career.

The training at West Point was a completely new world for one brought up in the wilds of the frontier, but he was a quick learner and with resolute determination he graduated in 1846, 17th in a class of 70 which contained men who were to serve as the leading generals in the Civil War, in both the Union and Confederate armies.

His first assignment was as a lieutenant in the Mexican War, under General Zachary Taylor, a fellow Virginian who became American President in 1849. He also fought in the Seminole Indian War in Florida and was elevated to Major. However, Jackson moved away from the front line of battle in 1851 when he accepted a teaching position at the Virginia Military Institute in Lexington and although still technically in soldiering, this brought him back into civilian life. The 10 years in Lexington was perhaps the most crucial period of his life and there he was to build a solid base for his later affray at the head of Virginia troops in the Civil War.

Although born into a Presbyterian family, Jackson had very little religious grounding as a youth and during his early Army career. This changed when he met Colonel Francis Taylor, the commandant of his regiment in Mexico and a committed Christian. "Stonewall" studied the Bible for himself and curiosity about various religions even led him to the Roman Catholic archbishop of Mexico for guidance. However, he was not convinced of the validity of Roman Catholic doctrines and in 1849 he was baptised at the age of 25, into the Episcopal Church, the American branch of Anglicanism.

In Lexington, it was the Presbyterian Church - the creed of his pioneering forebears which provided him with spiritual satisfaction and he made his profession of faith as a dissenting Calvinist in November, 1851. Soon after he became an elder of the church, and a lay preacher with a crusading zeal to win souls for Christ.

"Stonewall" married Eleanor Jenkins, daughter of the Rev. George Jenkins, president of Washington College in Virginia in 1854, but she died 14 months into the marriage. His second marriage in 1857, was to Mary Anna Morrison, daughter of Rev. Dr. R. H. Morrison, President of Davidson College in North Carolina. They had one daughter.

Religion became the main pre-occupation for "Stonewall" in those Lexington years and he took the Bible as his guide, literally interpreting every word on its pages. He was strict Sabbatarian - never reading a letter on that day, nor posting one; he believed that the federal government in carrying the mail on Sundays was violating a divine law. He was a Presbyterian elder, who was sometimes called "the blue light elder" by his men. To the church he gave one-tenth of his income, established a Sunday School from his own means and was particularly compassionate about the plight of the black slave children. Jackson's faith transcended every action of his life. He started the day with a blessing and always ended it with thanks to God. He said: "I have long cultivated the most trivial and customary acts of life with a silent prayer".

His two wives, during their marriages, were of similar Christian fundamentalist outlook, both daughters of a Presbyterian manse. Eleanor Jenkin's father was of Scottish Covenanting stock, who had come from Ulster in the late 18th century. The Morrisons were also of Scots-Irish extraction.

Whatever his standing at the Lexington Military College, Thomas Jonathan Jackson was not a wealthy man - he depended solely on his salary and both his wives were also of limited means. But he still managed to extend traditional Virginian hospitality to all who came in contact with him.

The outbreak of Civil War in April, 1861 and seceding of Virginia from the Union was a turning point in "Stonewall" Jackson's career and, at 37, he was called into action in the uniform of the Confederate Army. He was commissioned a colonel and took a detachment of Virginia Military Institute cadets from Lexington to Richmond to defend the Confederate flank there. Very soon he was in command of the Virginia forces at Harper's Ferry, a posting that placed him in the front line.

In July 1861, Jackson earned his stripes in the Battle of Bull Run at Manassas, inflicting a crushing defeat on the Union Army. The commander of the South Carolina Confederate, General Bernard E. Bee cried out to his men to look to Jackson, saying: "There he stands like a stone wall. Rally behind the Virginians". Bee, a classmate of Jackson from West Point, was to lose his life in the battle.

Jackson further distinguished himself at the second Battle of Bull Run in August, 1862. After marching 51 miles in two days, his "foot cavalry" smashed the Union depot at Manassas, went underground for another two days and then held off superior forces until Confederate reinforcements could be called. He had also notable battle success at Harper's Ferry, Antietam/ Sharpsbury and Fredericksburg.

The Battle of Chancellorsville on May 2, 1863 was sadly to be the last stand for "Stonewall", but the contribution he and his men made ensured victory for General Lee, although, with lack of money and resources, the tide was ominously turning against the Confederacy.

For his heroics at Bull Run, Jackson was commissioned Major-General and placed in charge of the Confederate Army in the Lower Shenandoah Valley. His soldiers referred to him as "Old Jack" and his tall, thin frame and long beard belied his barely 40 years. He was a man of puritan tastes: a non-smoker, a non-drinker and a non-gambler and he ate sparingly. Whatever his role in the Confederacy, he looked on war as "the sum of all evil", but in uniform he was a stern disciplinarian and made great demands on his men.

With General Robert E. Lee, the chief military advisor to the Confederacy President Jefferson Davis, Jackson moved to attack the Federal forces in the Valley and while they had reversals they managed to hold the line and send the Union Army retreating back to Washington.

"Stonewall" was the victim of mistaken fire by one of his own men. He lost an arm after being struck three times and was forced to retire from the battlefield. Death came quick when he contracted pneumonia and his last words, in a state of fever on May 10, 1863, were: "Pass the infantry to the front". He was only 39 when he died. General Lee had lost his first soldier and commented: "I know not how to replace him". Jackson's parting words were testimony of his abiding faith: "Let us cross over the river and rest under the shade of the trees".

Thomas Jonathan "Stonewall" Jackson was much respected even by his enemies on the Union side for his heroism, bravery, devotion to duty and purity of character. He was the true Christian patriot and President Abraham Lincoln, whose death was to come within two years, described him as "a very brave soldier".

Historians ponder on what might have happened in the Civil War had "Stonewall" Jackson not been killed. Serious reversals in the Shenandoah and at Gettysburg sealed the fate of the Confederacy for without the sterling leadership qualities of the redoubtable "Stonewall" the Johnny Rebs were never the same potent force again. Economic factors also mitigated against the Confederate cause.

"Stonewall" Jackson, great grandson of John Jackson, the pioneering emigrant from Ulster, was a soldier of special quality and steel. His soldiering exploits were in the best tradition of the Scots-Irish.

GENERAL ULYSSES SIMPSON GRANT

Ulysses Simpson Grant, the commander of the Union Army during the Civil War and the 18th President of the United States, is of third generation Ulster stock from Dergenagh near Dungannon in Co. Tyrone.

Grant's great-grandfather John Simpson left the north of Ireland for America in 1760 and after passing through Pennsylvania and Virginia the family eventually settled in Ohio, where the soldier/politician was born at Point Pleasant in 1822.

Ulysses graduated from West Point in 1843 and he saw military action in Missouri, Louisiana and Mexico, where he earned a citation for bravery.

When the Civil War started he was assigned in the Union Army as colonel of an Illinois volunteer infantry regiment and within a few months had risen to brigadier general. He earned his spurs in the Kentucky/Tennessee campaign of 1862, capturing Fort Henry and Fort Donelson from the Confederates. At Shiloh, in April of that year, his regiment sustained a lot of casualties, but they recovered and drove the Confederates from the field. Abraham Lincoln, rejecting calls for Grant's dismissal, said at the time: "I can't spare this man. He fights".

Grant, a shy retiring man of changing moods, turned out to be a bold strategist in the field of battle and he skilfully turned the War in favour of the Federal cause with significant successes at Vicksburg on the Mississippi River and at Chattanooga in Tennessee.

In March, 1864, Lincoln appointed Grant commander-in-chief of the Union Army and the final assault began against a waning Confederate force. Grant moved on Virginia where General Robert E. Lee was based, while his successor in Tennessee, W. T. Sherman, marched into Georgia towards Atlanta.

The August 23-27, 1776 edition of the Belfast News Letter announcing the news that the American Declaration of Independence had been signed on July 4, 1776.

The Conestoga Wagon, a favoured mode of travel by the 18th century Scots-Irish in America.

The remains of the home of the first Staunton, Virginia settler, Donegal-born John Lewis.

The bronze plaque of the graveside at Appomattox County, Virginia of James and Mary Bell McReynolds, both natives of Co. Tyrone who pioneered the American frontier.

The log house built by Joseph McReynolds in the 1790s at Rees Valley, Russell County, Virginia. His father Robert, who was born on the Atlantic Ocean when his Ulster-born parents, Joseph and Sarah Dixon McReynolds, were travelling to America, died in this house.

Luminaries of the Shenandoah Valley

General JEB Stuart

*General Thomas Jonathan
"Stonewall" Jackson*

*President Woodrow Wilson
(1856-1924)*

*General Sam Houston, Governor
of Tennessee and Texas.*

Cyrus McCormick, inventor of the grain reaper

Hay-making, Ulster style, at the Museum of American Frontier Culture at Staunton, Virginia.

The traditional Ulster farm cottage of the 18th century and outhouses at the Museum of American Frontier Culture at Staunton, Virginia.

Timber Ridge Presbyterian Church, Rockbridge County, Virginia.

*The grave of Ulster-Scots settler John Mackey at Timber Ridge
Presbyterian Church in the Shenandoah Valley.*

*Augusta Church, built
in 1755 - from the
Historical Atlas of
Augusta County 1888
Joseph A. Waddell/Jed
Hotchkiss.*

The typical house furnishings of a prosperous Scots-Irish settler in Tennessee and Virginia, as preserved by Dick Doughty of Greeneville in East Tennessee, home town of President Andrew Johnson.

Getting ready for the Transatlantic voyage at the Ulster American Folk Park near Omagh, Co. Tyrone.

Pioneering scene at the Ulster American Folk Park near Omagh, Co. Tyrone.

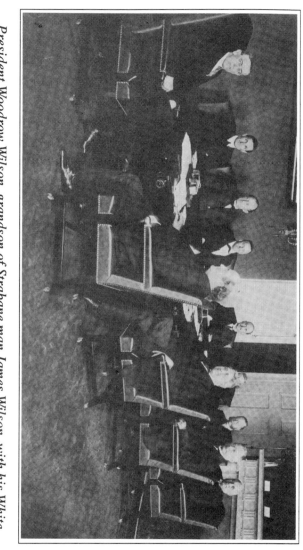

President Woodrow Wilson, grandson of Strabane man James Wilson, with his White House Cabinet of 1913. Third from left is James Clark McReynolds, the Attorney General and a direct descendant of the McReynolds family who moved from Killyman, South East Tyrone to Virginia in 1737.

*A typical Scots-Irish pioneering family entering the
Shenandoah Valley - David Wright (Artist), Nashville.*

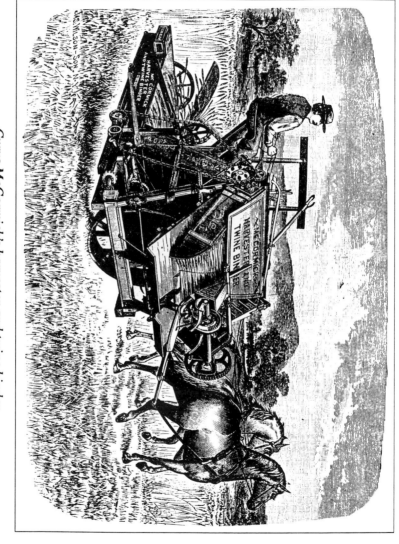

Cyrus McCormick's harvester and twine binder.
Historical Atlas of Augusta County 1888. Joseph A. Waddell/Jed Hotchkiss.

109

Appalachian-style music - Charlie Acuff on fiddle, Carl Bean on acoustic guitar, John Rice Irwin on mandolin and Carlock Stooksbury on Jew's harp.

110

Moonshining in the Blue Ridge Mountains of Virginia 30 years ago.

*The Crockett Tavern Museum, the boyhood home of Davy Crockett,
at Morristown, East Tennessee.*

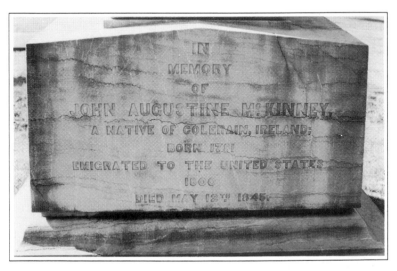

*The gravestone in Rogersville of distinguished East Tennessee lawyer
John Augustine McKinney who emigrated from Coleraine,
Co. Londonderry in 1800.*

112

President Bill Clinton and his wife Hillary receive a copy of 'The Scots-Irish in the Hills of Tennessee' from Belfast's Lord Mayor Councillor Eric Smyth at Belfast City Hall in November 1995.

Over the summer of 1864, Grant and Lee clashed in bloody battles at The Wilderness, Spotsylvania, Cold Harbor and Petersburg, with both armies losing tens of thousands of men. The last campaign for Grant came in the spring of 1865 and with the help of General Philip Sheridan he managed to outflank Lee's men in the Shenandoah Valley. The War was effectively at an end and Grant offered Lee generous terms of surrender, including the proviso that Confederate officers and men would be paroled and allowed home to their various Southern states. Lee signed the surrender document at Appomattox Court House on April 9 and over the summer Grant supervised the dismantling of the Union Army.

In 1868, Grant accepted the Republican nomination for the Presidency and without much electioneering he won an overwhelming victory, and in 1873 managed to hold on for another term. He died in 1885 after suffering from a painful throat cancer.

THE GALLANT "JEB" STUART OF THE CONFEDERACY

Heroic Confederacy Army General James Ewell Brown ("JEB") Stuart was the great, great grandson of Londonderry man Archibald Stuart, who emigrated to Pennsylvania in 1726 and became one of the leading citizens in the Shenandoah Valley of Virginia in the early settlements there. JEB Stuart was as daring a Confederate soldier as fought in the American Civil War and, with command of the cavalry of Northern Virginia, he enjoyed the confidence of his superiors General Robert E. Lee and General Thomas "Stonewall" Jackson.

After his military training at West Point, JEB Stuart rose from second lieutenant to Major General and, for one so young, he showed outstanding leadership qualities and courage far beyond the call of duty. He was the youngest Major-General in any army since the days of Napoleon Bonaparte and tragically was killed at the Battle of Yellow Tavern near Richmond.

JEB Stuart was born at Laurel Hill, Patrick County in the Shenandoah Valley, the seventh of 10 children of the Honourable Archibald Stuart, a leading Virginian lawyer, an officer in the Indian War of 1812 and a member of both the United States Congress and the Virginia legislature.

The Stuart family were strict Calvinists and pillars of the Presbyterian Church in the region and while JEB inherited a strong religious streak and remained an upholder of temperance throughout his army career, he had an aggressive character which on occasions led him into brawls and arguments with his peers and contemporaries. At West Point, outside of his studies, he was prone to fighting, very probably the fearless Scots-Irish instinct in his make-up, but despite this reputation, he graduated as officer material and quickly came to the attention of the Confederacy.

He served in Texas and Kansas and with Robert E. Lee in 1859 confronted John Brown, the radical slavery abolitionist, after Brown had led a raid on a United States armoury at Harper's Ferry in Virginia. In a bloody affray, 10 of the raiders were killed, Brown was injured, arrested and tried for treason. He was later hanged and this increased the bitterness between North and South, leading to the outbreak of the Civil War at Fort Sumter, South Carolina on April 12, 1861.

JEB Stuart, as a colonel of the First Virginia Cavalry, fought at Fort Manassas/Bull Run, and led his troops in the charge which secured a Confederate victory. He was promoted to brigadier general and set out the plans for the Virginia operation with a daring sojourn behind enemy lines for an assessment of Union strengths. This took him to the Potomac region and he returned to his Shenandoah Valley base with 165 prisoners and 260 captured horses.

Stuart was now a major general, commanding all the cavalry in Northern Virginia and in another foray into Union territory with 1,800 troopers, he returned with 500 captured horses. The daring exploits of JEB Stuart were the talk of the south and his men looked up to him for his fearlessness and willingness to take on any assignment which would advance the Confederate cause.

Stuart, a huge frame of a man with a flowing beard, led from the front, nearly always astride a magnificent charger. His dashing demeanour was manifest in his long grey coat, trimmed in red and a cavalier's cocked hat with a gilt star and a long peacock's plume. Socially, he was the life and soul of the party; loved music and dancing, but for all his jolifications he went to great lengths to discourage the consumption of alcohol.

Lee described JEB as "the eyes of the Confederate Army" and with the Union command he became a real thorn in the flesh, carrying out raid after raid on their posts and taking hundreds of prisoners back to the South. When "Stonewall" Jackson was killed at Chancellorsville in May, 1863, Stuart took over temporary command, but General Lee maintained he was irreplaceable as chief of cavalry and kept him in that position.

Stuart and his Virginia Cavalry continued to act as a buffer and intelligence unit for Lee's main army, but they had their set-backs, particularly at the Battle of Gettysburg, the real turning point in the Civil War.

Stuart's cavalry covered Lee's movements during the Wilderness Campaign of May 1864. He led 4,500 troopers in pursuit of the 12,000-strong Federal Cavalry Corps, under the command of Co. Cavan (Ireland) born General Philip Henry Sheridan. The Stuart unit reached Yellow Station on the Richmond Road and while they succeeded in moving the Union troops off the main route to Washington, Stuart was a casualty. He was shot in the abdomen and died in Richmond the following day.

General Lee in a tribute said: "He never brought me a false piece of information. He was a gallant soldier and a fine Southerner." JEB Stuart was married to Flora Cooke, daughter of Phillip Lt George Cooke, a general in the United States Army, but a native of Virginia. They had two children J.E.B. (James Ewell Brown) and Virginia Pelham.

The Stuarts were originally lowland Scots who settled in Londonderry as part of the Scottish Plantation of the 17th century. Archibald Stuart's people fought at the Siege of Londonderry in 1688-89, defending the city for the Protestant loyalist cause, and he sailed for Pennsylvania in 1726, to be followed a short time later by his wife Janet Brown and two young children, Thomas and Eleanor. Two other children, Alexander and Benjamin, were born in Pennsylvania and the family moved to Augusta County in the Shenandoah Valley in 1737.

Janet Brown's brother was the Rev. John Brown, who ministered at Providence Presbyterian Church in Rockbridge County for 44 years and became the second rector of Liberty Hall Academy, now Washington and Lee University.

Alexander Stuart was a major in the Virginian Militia during the Revolutionary War and distinguished himself at various battles. After the War, he acquired large properties throughout the Shenandoah and when he died, at the age of 90 in 1824, these were distributed among the 11 children of his three marriages. His family-inherited estate was at South River near Waynesborough.

Thomas Stuart inherited his father's main estate in Rockbridge and, quite appropriately, the large family Bible, which had been taken from

Ulster in 1726. Eleanor, Archibald's only daughter, married Edward Hall, who was also born in the north of Ireland and had moved to the Valley of Virginia with his family. She was given a tract of land at the South River. Benjamin Stuart was also given a farm, an indication of how prosperous Archibald Stuart had become by the time he ended his days in the Shenandoah.

Judge Alexander Stuart, a son of Major Alexander Stuart and Mary Moore Paxton (Stuart's second marriage), was a lawyer, a member of the executive council of Virginia, and a United States judge in Illinois and Missouri. He died in Staunton, Virginia in 1832 and is buried at Trinity Churchyard beside his half-brother Judge Archibald Stuart, from the marriage of Major Stuart and Mary Patterson. Judge Alexander Stuart married Anne Dabney, from a family of French immigrants, and they had a son, Archibald and daughter Anne.

This Archibald Stuart, born in Patrick County, in 1795, was the father of James Ewell Brown Stuart and had four sons and six daughters. The other members of this family succeeded in business in Virginia and sur-rounding states, and were leaders in the church and in civic and political life.

Mary Taylor Carter Stuart, a sister-in-law of JEB's through her mar-riage to Alexander Stuart, died in her early thirties from a camp fever she contracted while nursing wounded Confederate soldiers at Emory and Henry College in Virginia, which had been converted into an army hospital.

Alexander Hugh Holmes Stuart, a son of Judge Archibald Stuart and Eleanor Briscoe, was selected to the American Congress in 1841, but at the end of his first time term he decided that the 1,100 dollars a year, which was the going rate for Congressmen at that time, was a luxury he could not afford. He did not run for re-election, but in 1851 was ap-pointed Secretary of the Interior and was offered a diplomatic mission to Canada, but declined. He spent 16 years in the Virginia state legisla-ture.

Stuart is today an illustrious name in the Shenandoah Valley and be-yond in the adjoining Appalachian states. From the line of the original pioneer Archibald Stuart they have been trail-blazers in all stratas of society and the Scots-Irish legacy they have planted on the frontier has been an important ingredient in the shaping of America. JEB Stuart was undoubtedly the most distinguished of the family line.

GENERAL JOSEPH EGGLESTON JOHNSTON

This Virginian from Prince Edward County, was the son of a Revolutionary War veteran of Ulster stock. He graduated from West Point in 1829 and entered the Army as a second lieutenant of artillery.

Johnston fought in the various battles in Florida, Mexico, Kansas, Texas and Utah and by 1861, at the start of the Civil War he was a brigadier general and chief quartermaster of the American Army. He resigned his US commission and joined the Confederation Army as a major general.

Alongside Thomas "Stonewall" Jackson he played a key role in the Battle of Bull Run in 1861 and was given command of the Confederate Army at Richmond. He was ranked fourth in seniority in the Confederate Army and early in the war was a constant thorn in the flesh of the Union forces, led by another Ulster-Scot, General George B. McClellan.

Johnston was wounded at the Battle of Seven Pines in 1862 and lost his command to General Robert E. Lee. He returned later that year to supervise the army in Tennessee and Mississippi, but a succession of defeats brought disfavour from Confederacy President Jefferson Davis and he was relieved of his command shortly before the war ended. Johnston returned to field command in the Carolinas, but by this time the cause was lost. After the war, Johnston served a term in the United States Congress. He died in 1891, aged 84.

GENERAL DAVID McMURTRIE GREGG

This Pennsylvanian of Co. Antrim stock was a West Point-trained cavalryman and a veteran Indian fighter. He commanded various Union Army cavalry units during the Civil War and he was commended for repelling a Confederate attack led by General J.E.B. Stewart at Gettysburg in July, 1863.

GENERAL GEORGE BRINTON McCLELLAN

This senior Union officer was the son of a Philadelphia surgeon, whose Ulster-Scots family fought alongside fellow Virginian General George Washington in the Revolutionary War. George McClellan, another West Point graduate and a Mexican War veteran, from the same class as

Thomas Jonathan "Stonewall" Jackson, studied military tactics in Europe and one of his works was a report on the Siege of Sebastopol.

In the decade before the Civil War he worked as an engineer and administrator for the railway companies in Illinois, Ohio and Mississippi. When War broke out in 1861, he was commissioned a major general of the Ohio Volunteers and he saw early action against the Confederates in Western Virginia.

McClellan's prowess as a soldier, organiser and administrator was admired by President Abraham Lincoln and he was authorised to reverse the set-back suffered at the Battle of Bull Run in 1861. He successfully strengthened the Washington defences and in Virginia, but found General Robert E. Lee and his Confederates a tough obstacle at Richmond in May/June 1862 and was forced to retreat.

Abraham Lincoln demoted him to No.2 in favour of General John Pope, but after another defeat at the second Battle of Bull Run in August, 1862 he resumed command. McClellan, known to his men as "Little Mac" got a share of the spoils at Antietam Creek in Maryland, in November, 1862 but failed to stop the Confederates returning to Virginia and was removed for the last time by Lincoln. Robert E. Lee considered McClellan as the ablest Union commander he faced, but not managing a significant battle success his reputation on the Union side withered. McClellan, it was said, always wanted more men, more equipment, more time to plan. "George McClellan is an admirable engineer, but he seems to have a special talent for the stationary engine", said Abraham Lincoln.

McClellan was the Democratic candidate for the Presidency against Abraham Lincoln in 1864, but he won majority support in only three states and Lincoln was an overwhelming winner. For three years in 1878-81 McClellan served as Governor of New Jersey.

GENERAL IRVIN McDOWELL

Union General Irvin McDowell is believed to have been a descendant of Ulster emigrant Ephriam McDowell who settled in Augusta County in the Shenandoah Valley of Virginia in the mid-18th century. General McDowell was a graduate of West Point and fought during the Mexican War of the 1840s. He held several army assignments prior to the Civil War and in May 1861, at the outbreak of hostilities, he was promoted to brigadier general in charge of troops in Washington.

McDowell, who had never before held a field command, was thrown in at the deep end and he saw defeat for his forces at the Battle of Bull Run in July, 1861. He was superseded by another Ulster-Scot, General George McClellan and became a division commander, based in Washington. His performance in charge of Virginian troops at the second Battle of Bull Run in 1862 was heavily criticised and he was relieved of his commission. He retired to California and as a parks commissioner in San Francisco he is credited with laying out the roads in the Presidio which overlooks the Golden Gate.

GENERAL PHILIP HENRY SHERIDAN

This son of Co. Cavan immigrants, born in Albany, New York and grew up in Ohio, was one of the Union Army's most prolific officers. Sheridan, a West Point graduate, served in Texas and fought the Indians in the Pacific Northwest engagements.

In the Civil War he rose from being a quartermaster and commissary in the Southwest Army to colonel in charge of the 2nd Michigan Cavalry, which had battle successes over the Confederacy in Mississippi, Kentucky and Tennessee. He was promoted to major general and, under General Ulysses S. Grant, led the infantry charge at Missionary Ridge and Chattanooga.

In 1864 Grant appointed Sheridan as commander of the Cavalry corps of the Potomac Army and it was his forces who halted the Confederates, under General J.E.B. Stuart, at Yellow Tavern near Richmond. Stuart was killed in this battle and Sheridan followed up by routing the Confederate cavalry in four different engagements. Sheridan then went on a scorched earth campaign in the Shenandoah, riding from Winchester to thwart the remaining Confederate resistance in the War. It was claimed his soldiers burned 2,000 barns and 700 mills in Virginia and cut off all supplies to the rebel Army. He returned to help Grant corner Robert E. Lee in Northern Virginia and the inevitable surrender came on April 9, 1865.

A month after the War ended, Sheridan commanded an army of 50,000 Civil War veterans at the Rio Grande in a bid to remove the French from Mexican soil. He served as military governor of Texas and Louisiana, led campaigns against the Plains Indians and finished his military career with a four-year spell as commander-in-chief of the American Army. He died in 1888, only 57.

GENERAL JAMES SHIELDS

Unlike most of the other Civil War generals with Ulster roots General James Shields was a Roman Catholic, from Altmore, Pomeroy in Co. Tyrone. Shields, born in 1806, came to America as a 17-year-old and was a lawyer in Illinois.

Shields fought in the Indian and Mexican Wars and was involved in Democratic politics. He once challenged Abraham Lincoln to a duel over criticism in a newspaper article, but they settled their differences and became close friends. Before the Civil War, he was Governor of Oregon Territory and was a United States Senator for Illinois and Minnesota.

As a brigadier general in the Union Army, Shields served in the Shenandoah Valley campaign of 1862. He resigned his commission in 1863 and after a spell as railway commissioner in California, he had another term as a United States Senator, this time for Missouri, becoming the only person in American history to serve three different states in the Senate.

GENERAL DANIEL SMITH DONELSON

Confederate Army General Daniel Smith Donelson was a member of a Scots-Irish family from Co. Antrim who pioneered significant settlements in Tennessee during the latter part of the 18th century.

General Donelson (1801-63) was descended from John Donelson, who, with James Robertson, founded the city of Nashville in 1780 after he formed the Watauga settlement in the 1770s in a part of North Carolina which today is in East Tennessee. Rachel Donelson, John Donelson's daughter, married Andrew Jackson, the Tennessean politician/soldier who went on to become American President in 1828.

Daniel Smith Donelson was a West Point graduate, who enjoyed considerable influence in Tennessee as a planter, militiaman and democratic state legislator. He was an active secessionist who built Fort Donelson, while in the provisional army. As a Confederate brigadier general he led brigades in West Virginia and served under General Robert E. Lee at Charleston and General Braxton Bragg at Perryville, Stones River and Shelbyville. He was also commander of the East Tennessee Confederate forces.

LT. GENERAL LEONIDAS POLK

Another Confederate General, Leonidas Polk had links to the White House through his cousin James Knox Polk, who was the 11th United States President during the period 1845-49. The Polks were a well-placed Ulster Presbyterian family from the Londonderry/East Donegal region who moved to America in the early part of the 18th century.

Leonida's father fought in the Revolutionary War and he helped found the University of North Carolina, where his son studied for two years before entering West Point. During his fourth year there, Leonidas came under the influence of a chaplain, was converted and set about training for the ministry in the Episcopal Church.

He was ordained a priest in May, 1831, served as assistant rector of a Richmond, Virginia parish, but resigned after several years due to ill-health. He later returned to the church as missionary bishop of the south west, covering the states of Alabama, Mississippi, Louisiana and Arkansas.

In 1841, Polk became bishop of Louisiana and he settled on a large sugar plantation with 400 slaves, an inheritance of his wife. The bishop established a Sunday School for the slaves, but the plantation proved a financial failure. His Ashwood Hall home was one of the finest buildings in Tennessee. He returned full-time to the ministry and established the University of the South at Suwanee, Tennessee in October, 1860, aimed at educating the southern ruling class. His St. John's Parish Church in Middle Tennessee is today the oldest Episcopal Church in the state, a national historic monument. When the Civil War broke out in 1861 Polk was offered a major general's commission in the Confederate Army by Jefferson Davis, who had been a cadet with him at West Point. Polk, believing the South was fighting for a holy cause, readily accepted.

His first military assignment was in the defence of the Mississippi River and his troops occupied Columbus, Kentucky in September, 1861, an action which violated that state's neutrality and pushed it towards the Union cause. He became a corps commander with Albert Sidney Johnston, another close friend from West Point, and they fought together at Shiloh in April, 1862.

Polk was promoted to lieutenant general and saw action at Perryville, Stones River and Chickamuaga. However, Polk's soldiering techniques were open to much criticism from senior colleagues and so lax was he at

Chickamauga that he was recommended for court martial by his superior officer, General Braxton Bragg. This however, was over-ruled by Jefferson Davis. Polk was killed near Marietta, Georgia during the Atlanta campaign. He was blown out of his saddle by a shot fired from a parrott rifle cannon. He was 58.

BRIGADIER GENERAL CHARLES GRAHAM HALPINE

This north of Ireland born son of a Church of Ireland rector worked for the New York Times as their Washington correspondent and enlisted in the Union Army as a private at the start of the War in 1861.

Halpine fought in the various battles in Virginia and when he resigned his commission in 1864 he held the rank of Brigadier General. During the War he contributed to newspapers under the pen name of "Pvt. Miles O'Reilly." He became active after the War in the Democratic Party.

16

Mark Twain's *family ties to the Scots-Irish*

S amuel Langhorn Clemens, who gained worldwide acclaim as the author Mark Twain, was directly linked to the Scots-Irish on both sides of his family.

Revolutionary War hero Colonel William Casey and his wife Jane Montgomery Casey were the grandparents of Jane Lampton Clemens, Samuel Langhorn's mother, and both belonged to families who emigrated to America from Ulster in the mid-18th century. Colonel Casey became a prominent landowner after the war and is credited with founding two Kentucky states, Greensburg and Columbia. He lived in both Virginia and Tennessee and is believed to have been at the Battle of Kings Mountain in October, 1780 along with kinsmen Levi and Randolph Casey.

John Marshall Clemens, Mark Twain's father, was born at Bedford County in the Shenandoah Valley in a family with roots in Co. Antrim. John's father died when he was only seven while helping a neighbour to build a log cabin and his mother remarried. The family moved to Adair County, Kentucky, where John was licensed to practise law and he married Jane Lampton, the daughter of Benjamin and Peggy Casey Lampton, a couple who had pioneered a wild and remote region at Cherry Creek, deep in the Cumberland Mountains of Tennessee. It was here that John and Jane Clemens lived before they moved to Missouri and their son Samuel Langhorn was born in 1835.

Under the pseudonym of Mark Twain, Clemens became a novelist, short story writer and humourist. His childhood growing up in the wilds of Missouri were recalled in The Adventures of Tom Sawyer (1876) and The Adventures of Huckleberry Finn (1884). He worked as a printer, and as a pilot on the Mississippi River steamers. The pen name Mark Twain was taken from the riverboat term, meaning safe water of two fathoms.

Clemens headed west to Nevada and California, where he developed a journalistic career, and he travelled to Europe and the Middle East on various lecture tours. The Huckleberry Finn story of a boy and an escaped black slave travelling down the Mississippi River in the pre-Civil War south era gave him international prominence and tested the conscience of the American public on the slavery issue that lingered long after the abolition.

Samuel Langhorn Clemens, a wealthy but highly complex man, died in 1910, aged 74, heartbroken by the death of his two daughters and the long illness and death of his wife.

17

Cyrus McCormick's *inventive skills*

Cyrus Hall McCormick, the man who invented an agricultural reaping machine that revolutionised grain harvesting in the United States, came of an Ulster-Scots Presbyterian family who settled in the Shenandoah Valley.

McCormick, born in 1809, was reared on a farm in Rockbridge County close to Lexington and from an early age he was obsessed with experimenting on the tools of the land. In 1831, he built his first reaper and tested the machine on the wheat and oats of his father Robert's farm. By 1840, Cyrus, with the help of his brothers, had perfected the reaper as a saleable commodity in Virginia and within a few years had expanded the market to other parts of the United States.

The horse-drawn reaper enabled farmers to harvest more than 10 acres of grain a day, quite an advance from the two to three acres achieved via the hand scythe method. It was an invention which really caught the imagination of farmers across the American nation and when his business expanded, McCormick moved to Chicago in 1847. There he used the Great Lakes of the Mid-West to transport the reapers to the Eastern states, and the Mississippi River to the territories of the South, and into Canada.

The advent of the railways boosted trade and by the early 1850s the McCormick Harvesting Machine Company was listed as the largest farm implement factory in the world. McCormick remained president of the multi-million dollar company until his death in 1884 and by 1902 the concern had merged to become the International Harvester Company, under his son Cyrus Jun. The enterprising Cyrus McCormick, possessed with enthusiasm, inventive genius and commercial ability, also established the McCormick Theological Seminary and was also engaged in real estate, mining and railroading interests.

His humble ancestors had moved to the Shenandoah Valley from the north of Ireland in the mid-18th century and prospered at Rockbridge County. In Northern Ireland today the McCormick or McCormack family link is very strong, right across the Province. Cyrus McCormick is remembered at an exhibition in the ancestral home of President Ulysses Simpson Grant's great grandfather John Simpson at Dergenagh near Dungannon in Co. Tyrone. It is claimed the McCormick family lived near the Simpsons in Co. Tyrone.

18

Scots-Irish families *of the Shenandoah*

THE ALEXANDERS

Archibald Alexander emigrated from Ireland with his wife Margaret Parks and infant daughter in 1736 and after 11 years living in Chester County, Pennsylvania, they moved to Rockbridge County in the Shenandoah Valley at South River opposite the mouth of the Irish Creek.

The Alexanders were part of the Scottish Plantation of Ulster in the early 17th century and it was Archibald's grandfather (of the same name) who founded the homestead at Manorcunningham in Co. Donegal. Archibald was Donegal-born in 1708 and he married his cousin Margaret Parks in 1734.

Like nearly all of the early settlers of Rockbridge County, Archibald Alexander was a farmer, but living on the dangerous American frontier he was commissioned into the military service and fought in the French and Indian Wars of the 1750s/1760s period. He captained a company of Rangers at the Sandy Creek expedition and for this service he received several thousand acres of land in Kentucky.

Archibald, who was an elder in Timber Ridge Presbyterian Church, was married twice. Margaret Parks died in 1753 and four years later Archibald married Jane McClure, of Rockbridge County. He had seven children by the first marriage, eight by the second - the Scots-Irish settlers were good breeders. Elizabeth, the infant daughter born in Ireland, married Rockbridge County farmer John McClung, who was also Irish-born. They had ten children.

There are records of other Alexanders moving from Ulster to Pennsylvania in the 18th century, settling in Chester and Lancaster Counties. George Alexander, who emigrated with his wife Jane in 1745, had all his 10 sons listed as Revolutionary War soldiers in the North Carolina militia. Captain William Alexander served with the 4th North Carolina Regiment and in 1797 settled his family in Greene County in East Tennessee.

Eight Alexanders are listed as patriots at the Battle of Kings Mountain in October, 1780: Aiken Alexander, Daniel Alexander, Elias Alexander, Jeremiah Alexander, John Alexander, Oliver Alexander, James Alexander and Joseph Alexander. The latter was born in Co. Antrim in 1759 and lived at Spartanburg in North Carolina. A family connection with the Alexanders, of Rockbridge County has not been established.

THE ARMSTRONGS

The Armstrong family, of Co. Fermanagh (Ulster) stock, were closely associated with the Presbyterian congregation of Tinkling Spring in Augusta County, Virginia. The family left Brookeborough in Co. Fermanagh in the late 1730s/early 1740s.

Armstrong is still a very common name in Augusta County, Virginia and in East Tennessee, many of the clan probably tracing their ancestry back to William Armstrong, who was born in Fermanagh in 1712 and who, in his later years, lived in Hawkins County, Tennessee, to the advanced age of 103.

The New Providence Presbyterian Church, the oldest church in Tennessee in continuous existence from 1780, was founded in the home of William Armstrong, whose wife was Mary Caldwell from Ireland. A second William Armstrong is recorded as having served at the Battle of Kings Mountain, the Battle of Cowpens and was at Charleston when the British left. He is listed as born in Ireland in 1765.

Another Armstrong family, headed by Robert and Alice Calhoun, left Ulster in 1735 and, after staying in Pennsylvania for seven years, headed in the direction of South Carolina. Robert I never made the full journey to the frontier - he died at Augusta County, Virginia in 1754, but his children carried on, eventually settling at Abbeville, South Carolina. Robert II was a lieutenant in the 1st South Carolina Regiment during the

Revolutionary War and in 1784 was living in Washington County, North Carolina (today Tennessee).

His final home was five miles east of Knoxville on the Holston/French Board Rivers. A nephew Robert Houston (son of Alice Armstrong) was the first sheriff of Knox County and later was Tennessee Secretary of State under Governors William Blount and John Sevier and a Tennessee state senator.

Robert Houston, described as tall, muscular and a graceful man, had energy, thrift and intelligence, common to his Scots-Irish kinsfolk. He later became paymaster to the East Tennessee troops and was commissioner in the treaty completed with the Cherokees, the brainchild of John C. Calhoun, the then Secretary of War. John C's grandfather, Patrick Calhoun, was a brother of Robert Armstrong I's wife, Alice.

The descendants of James Armstrong, another family bearing the name, were extensive farmers in Orange County, North Carolina from the first settlement there in the 1750s.

James (1701-1796) was Ulster-born and moved to Pennsylvania in the first wave of the Scots-Irish. He married Mollie Bird and they had six children. In 1755 Armstrong purchased 607 acres of land in Orange County for £29-12-0 (twenty nine pounds, twelve shillings) and later extended his holdings with more purchases.

William Armstrong, a son, married Jane Lapsley, of Ulster-Scots stock from Virginia, and after his wife's death took a commission as ensign with the 1st North Carolina Battalion in the Revolutionary War. He became a captain and for his service received a land grant of 3,840 acres in Davidson County in Middle Tennessee. He later settled in Hawkins County, East Tennessee.

THE BELLS

Shenandoah settler Joseph Bell was one of several brothers whose father emigrated from the North of Ireland in the 1730s. He came to Augusta County from Lancaster County in Pennsylvania in 1740 and married Elizabeth Henderson, who was also of Scots-Irish Presbyterian stock.

Joseph Bell helped in the construction of the Old Stone Church at Augusta and was a leading member of the congregation. His son James Bell was a magistrate of Augusta County for many years from 1796 and served on the state legislature. Other members of the Bell family settled in Tennessee, Ohio, and Kentucky and a descendant was the Hon. John Bell, of Tennessee, who was a candidate for the American Presidency against Abraham Lincoln in 1860 on the Whig ticket. John Bell, born near Nashville, was a lawyer who served 14 years in the U.S. House of Representatives, one year as speaker; as War Secretary in 1841, and a Senator for 12 years.

THE BOLLARS

Ulster-born John Bollar emigrated to Pennsylvania where he lived near Brandywine Manor, Chester County. He settled in southwest Bath County, Virginia on the Jackson River about an eighth of a mile above the point where Mill Creek joins the river. He was a large landowner and his home, a log house, was one of the first in the area.

John replaced his home in 1792 with a larger house, carving the date in the chimney. This house with additions and improvements was destroyed by a fire in 1942. The land remained in the family until it was sold about 1930. It was later acquired by the State of Virginia and was flooded in the 1970s when the Gathright Dam was built. The graves at the old homestead were moved to the Warm Springs Cemetery.

John Bollar served as a regular soldier in frontier defence during the French and Indian War of the 1750s/1760s. When Botetourt County was formed from Augusta in 1770, he was commissioned a justice by the royal governor in 1769 and served the new county between 1770 and 1777. He was an elder in Botetourt Church and a captain in the new county militia. During the Revolutionary War he served in 1881 with the Virginia Militia at Reedy Fork and Guilford Courthouse battles. When Bath County was formed he was one of the original justices and he was sheriff in 1792.

He married Margaret Thornton in 1744, and they had eleven children. The Bollars are buried at the family homestead on the Jackson River.

THE CALLISONS

This family from Co. Armagh in Ulster were part of a large Scots-Irish migration to Pennsylvania and then to the Shenandoah Valley of

Virginia in the 1740s. The Callisons, originally Quakers, had been lease-holders in the townlands of Ballyloughan, Mullaghdry, Kilmore and Ballyhagan which today lies close to Richhill and Loughgall, about five miles from the ecclesiastical city of Armagh.

James Callison (born 1722) and his wife Isabella made the trek to America after their marriage in 1742 and it is recorded James came from Albemarle County, Virginia to Augusta County in 1745. There he acquired two plots of land totalling 556 acres, part of the Beverly Manor estate near the present-day town of Greenville.

James's younger sister, Margaret, who also emigrated, married in 1748 a Robert McCutcheon from Glasgow, Scotland. They had 12 children, all born in Virginia. James and Isabella Callison had seven daughters and four sons. The second daughter Isabella (born 1746) married in 1779 in Rockbridge County, George McNutt, born in mid-Co. Antrim, Ulster in 1751. George fought with the Revolutionary Army at the Battle of Kings Mountain in 1780 and by 1785 had left Virginia to become one of the first settlers in the 'Irish Bottom', south of the French Broad River in what became Jefferson County, Tennessee, about seven years later. A daughter, Jenny was born and was said to have been the first white child born south of the French Broad River. Altogether they had two sons and five daughters.

The McNutts had moved to a new farm near White's Fort on the Holston River which became part of Knox County. George was made town commissioner of Knoxville and a Justice of the Peace when Knox County was formed in 1792. He was an elder in First Knoxville Presbyterian Church, a charter trustee of both Blount College and Hampden Sidney Academy and a trustee of Washington College in Washington County, Tennessee. He died in 1823. Isabella's younger brother James Callison followed her and George McNutt to Tennessee and married Anne Gillespie in Knox County in 1794 before going to live in Roane County where he was known to be in 1809.

Another James Callison was the only son of five children born to Anthony Callison and Abigail (nee Wethereld), who lived in the townland of Mullalelish in the parish of Kilmore, Co. Armagh. James was born in 1739 and attended the Friends' Meeting House at Ballyhagan from where a certificate was issued on August 8, 1763 for transfer to another con-gregation when he was leaving for America.

He married an Elizabeth McCallister and on August 17, 1765 was admitted to the Quaker meeting at Burlington, New Jersey. Their first son Anthony was born at this time and Elizabeth had two more sons before she died in 1772. A land survey of 1774 shows James Callison holding 589 acres on the north side of Greenbrier River, Virginia.

James then married Mary, one of the daughters of James and Isabella Callison and they had a further three sons and five daughters. In September 1782 James obtained a warrant for 324 acres on the south side of Locust Creek, Greenbrier County; on January 9, 1787, grant of 370 acres at Locust Bottom; on October 16, 1787, 360 acres at Big Levels and on February 14, 1795, 35 acres and 118 acres at Little Levels.

In 1794, James's son Anthony married Abigail McClung, daughter of Charles McClung, one of the founding fathers of Knoxville, Tennessee. James Callison moved to Grainger County, Tennessee and obtained grant for 600 acres on south side of the Holston River.

The other James Callison, living in Augusta County, died in 1788 and his sons Jonathan and James got land grants in 1797 on the north side of Holston River in Grainger County. James got 300 acres, Jonathan 150 acres. A marriage bond dated July 17, 1800 to the State Governor of Tennessee, John Sevier in the sum of 3,000 dollars for the marriage of James Callison and Elizabeth Young is signed by James Callison Snr. and James Callison Jnr.

James Snr. may be the James whose first wife Elizabeth McCallister was the mother of their third son James, born 1770, who married Susannah Edmiston in 1797. Elisha, youngest child of James and his second wife Mary Callison was born in 1792. He inherited 360 acres at Big Levels, now Lewisburg in Virginia, served in the 2nd Regiment Virginia Militia in the 1812 War and was made Colonel. He served as a judge in County Court for 27 years, was commissioner of revenue for Greenbrier County, and representative in the Virginia Legislature 1845-6 and 1850-1. The census of 1850 had him farming 22,000 acres.

Elisha married Margaret (Peggy) Bright in 1821 and they had five sons and three daughters. One son Elisha Francis, graduated as a doctor from Virginia University Medical School in 1850. The youngest son William Henry Callison was a Confederate soldier in "Stonewall" Jackson's Brigade, 27th Virginia Infantry Company 'E'. He died on the battlefield at Manassas on July 21, 1861.

THE CAMPBELLS

The Campbells were in the vanguard of lowland Scots who settled in Ulster in the 17th century plantation and many of them made their way on to the American frontier. Colonel William Campbell, who led the Virginian militia at the Battle of Kings Mountain in 1780, was the most distinguished member of the clan, but there were others who made an outstanding contribution in settling townships and churches and in military service.

Captain Charles Campbell, born in Ulster in 1703, came to Augusta County, Virginia by way of Pennsylvania. His home was five miles north east of Staunton and he was a leading member of the Old Stone Presbyterian Church. A kinsman of the same name was an elder at New Providence Presbyterian Church, a militia officer in the French and Indian Wars, High Sheriff of Rockbridge County and a trustee of Washington College for 29 years. A son, Charles, wrote a history of Virginia in 1860.

John Campbell came from Ireland to America in 1726 with his family and settled first at Lancaster County, Pennsylvania. By 1738 he was in Augusta County with his three sons Patrick, Robert and David. A grandson of Patrick was Colonel William Campbell, of Kings Mountain fame, and when his father Charles died in 1767 the family moved to 1,000 acres at the Holston Valley settlement of East Tennessee (then in North Carolina).

THE COCHRANS

John Cochran, the father of this distinguished Shenandoah frontier family, was born in Co. Armagh in the north of Ireland about 1725 and he came to America with his two brothers Robert and James in 1745.

Robert and James remained in Pennsylvania, but John moved to Virginia settling on the William McCue farmlands, about two miles from Augusta Old Stone Presbyterian Church. John married Susannah Donnelly, who was also born in Co. Armagh and had emigrated to America with her aunt in 1745 upon the death of her parents. The family were strong Presbyterians.

John Cochran became a prominent merchant and magistrate at Staunton and owned a plantation at Fort Defiance, to the north of the town. It was recorded that by natural thrift and sound business ability he accumulated and left a handsome legacy for his children. His elder son James married Magdalen, a daughter of Colonel George Moffett, a Revolutionary War hero.

He died in 1765 and was buried in the older section of the Old Stone Church, where a marker reads: "Cochran - This stone marks the grave of John Cochran. Born in the County Armagh (Ireland), in 1725, he came to America in 1745, settled in the Old Stone Church neighbourhood where he lived until his death in 1765. He was a man of intelligence, high character and sterling worth, qualities which he transmitted to his innumerable descendants throughout the United States".

John Cochran II served in the Revolutionary War under Colonel George Moffett and was a wheelwright and joiner by trade. Along with his brother Robert he inherited much of his father's land.

Susannah Donnelly Cochran married again in 1768 to Henry King, of Maryland. A descendant is Judge George Moffett Cochran, of Staunton, Virginia, who today is one of the leading members of the Virginia judiciary. He is chairman of the Museum of American Frontier Culture at Staunton. Judge Cochran and his wife Lee Stuart were selected as the 1995 'Outstanding Virginian', the first time a couple has been chosen for this prestigious award. Now retired, Judge Cochran served on the bench as Virginia Supreme Court Justice for 18 years and is still called on for judicial duties on an interim basis. He was also a member of Virginia's Senate and his wife Lee Stuart, a descendant of American Civil War general J.E.B. Stuart, has served on numerous state boards and commissions in Virginia.

THE COXS

Joshua and Mary (Rankin) Cox were Ulster immigrants who were in Lancaster County, Pennsylvania in the 1730s. A son John was a captain under General George Washington's command in Virginia before and during the Revolutionary War. He marched against Cornstalk, the Shawnee Indian chieftain, at the Battle of Point Pleasant in 1774 in what was known as Dunnore's War and later, in 1780, fought at the Battle of Kings Mountain along with George, Joseph and William Cox.

After the war John Cox bought and established a plantation of 3,000 acres at Ashe and Allegheny Counties in North Carolina and he also received extensive land grants in Tennessee for services rendered.

THE CRAWFORDS

Patrick Crawford, who emigrated from Ulster to Pennsylvania in the 1740s, was the first of the family in America and he settled at Augusta County in the Shenandoah in 1750.

He had three sons - William, James and John - and his descendants were some of the foremost citizens in Augusta County for more than two centuries. Patrick, a man of sound sense, great energy and persevering industry, accumulated a large estate.

THE CROZIERS

John Crozier, merchant and postmaster in Knoxville, Tennessee in the early 19th century, was a Co. Fermanagh (Ulster) man who emigrated to America in 1785. His father John had been a prominent citizen in Ulster, holding the position of High Sheriff of Fermanagh in 1765.

John, the emigrant, lived for a period at Abingdon, Virginia, but by 1796 he was a partner in a mercantile company in Knoxville. In the same year he was commissioned by Governor John Sevier as captain of the cavalry volunteers of the Knox County militia.

He was made deputy postmaster of Knoxville in 1798 and became postmaster in 1804. He held this office until his death in 1838 and during his term main routes for carrying the mail in East Tennessee were established.

Crozier, a solid Presbyterian and strong educationalist, was a trustee of Blount College and was one of three commissioners tasked with the overseeing of the building of First Knoxville Presbyterian Church. He had business interests in the Knoxville Water Company and the Bank of Tennessee and became a man of great wealth and influence. A son John H. Crozier was a member of the bar in Tennessee and was twice elected to the United States House of Representatives. Another son, Arthur R. Crozier was comptroller of the treasury of Tennessee.

THE DITTYS

John Ditty, the blacksmith, was a Revolutionary War soldier who lived in various settlements in Pennsylvania, Virginia and Tennessee. He was born in 1756, of Ulster-born parents and served with the Lancaster County, Pennsylvania militia.

After the war he moved to Virginia and ran an ordinary (a licensed tavern) in the town of Christianburg, Montgomery County. In June, 1799 he was appointed road overseer in Montgomery County and in the 1810 census he was listed as living in Wyeth County, Virginia, an adjoining state. John's next move was to Tennessee and it was near the town of Cookeville that he carried on a blacksmith's shop. He died in 1846 aged 90, after this some members of the family moved to new lands in Missouri and Oregon.

THE GILLESPYS (GILLESPIES)

This family were originally lowland Scots from Kirkcudbright who after several years farming on the hillsides of Co. Antrim headed across the Atlantic for a new life on the American frontier.

James and Jennet Gillespy landed with their daughter Agnus and sons John, James and William at Philadelphia on July 24, 1740 and within a short period had settled on the Beverley Manor lands at Augusta County in Virginia. Two other daughters Margaret and Elizabeth were born in Virginia, but Margaret died at infancy. James Sen., helped found the Tinkling Spring Presbyterian Church in 1741, verified by an inscription on a monument in the churchyard.

Confirmation of the family's short period of life in Ulster comes from the fact that Agnus, John and James Gillespy were born in Scotland in the 1731-35 period. William was born in Ireland in 1737.

James fought in the Indian Wars with the Virginia militia and his three sons took part in the Revolutionary War, before moving on to new land holdings at Blount County in East Tennessee, then Green County, North Carolina. James Jnr., who served in the War with the Third Virginia Regiment of the Continental Army, acquired 150 acres and his brother John 450 acres about 1787. This was largely Indian territory and in October, 1788 hostile tribesmen attacked the Gillespy fort while some of the men were away. Several people, including James Gillespy, son of John, were massacred and some taken captive. Five years later there was another serious Indian attack on the Gillespy fort, which resulted in the death of James and one of his sons and the capture of another, who was freed a month later on ransom payment of a quantity of leather and a horse.

John Gillespy, the oldest son, had 10 children and owned land at Virginia, Tennessee and Kentucky. After his brother's untimely death, he looked after the welfare of his nephews and nieces.

James Gillespy, son of James Jun. and known as "Smoking Jimmy", became a magistrate in Blount County, a member of the Tennessee legislature and a prominent Presbyterian elder. His son, James Houston Gillespy, was an eminent physician of his day, who graduated from the Jefferson Medical College in Philadelphia and over a period acquired 20,000 acres of mountain and forest land in East Tennessee. He was a man of many parts, fiercely independent in the Scots-Irish mould and possessed with an inherent dislike of federal government.

At the time of the American Civil War, Dr. James Houston Gillespy, was Postmaster at Maryville in East Tennessee and while holding this position he became involved in a rather bizarre affair for a man of his age, and standing in the community. He was persuaded by John H. Reagon, a cabinet colleague of Confederate Government leader Jefferson Davis, to go to Charleston, South Carolina and rob a branch of the United States Treasury.

Gillespy was joined by a group of vigilantes and, on successful completion of the operation, they handed over a sizeable amount of money to Reagon, who conveyed it to Jefferson Davis for use in the Confederate cause. The doctor was arrested, tried and convicted of treason, which was then punishable by the death penalty. However, he was given a pardon at the end of the Civil War in 1867 after correspondence between himself and President Andrew Johnson, the former Mayor of Greeneville in East Tennessee. Had the affair not occurred during the Civil War period, Gillespy and his family would most certainly have been scandalised, but in Confederate minds what he and the vigilantes did was considered a patriotic act.

The letter, sent by Dr. James Houston Gillespy to President Johnson on November 27, 1866, read: "My object in writing this is to be restored to citizenship; and I am told the President's Pardon is necessary to that end as I have civil offices under the Confederate Government. I am 67 years of age, son of James Gillespy, of Little River, Blount County. By profession a physician and for the last 40 years, when able, practiced my profession. In 1860, I was elected County Registrar. Continued to hold and fill the office after Tennessee seceded from the Union. I likewise was appointed and filled the office of Postmaster for a short time under the Southern Confederacy. For the last 30 years held the opinion that free slave states could not live together in harmony under one constitution. I doubted not, but the whole Union would be visited by a judgment on the account of abscess of slavery, of which neither North nor South can claim to be free from guilt. I now rejoice to know that we are free from slavery and dread the danger of running into the opposite extreme. And feel anxious to be enabled to throw in my mite to stop the current that is fast flowing to the gulf of anarchy. And I must say that your consistently able if masterly action in endeavouring to stop the tide of radicalism has encouraged and delighted me. And I can say that I know not that I have personal enemy either amongst the Union or rebel citizens. These have been my actions and goals and if it would be consistent with the proper duties of your office to grant me that pardon the law requires you would greatly oblige your obedient, humble servant".

As a doctor, James Houston Gillespy, was highly regarded, even by the native American people, and it is recorded that he was given a tract of land by an Indian chief for curing his wife of an illness. His youngest son, Dr. Samuel Tucker Gillespy, was a senior officer and surgeon of the Confederate forces in East Tennessee.

Ulster-born William Gillespy, another son of the original pioneering couples James and Jennet, ran a ferry crossing on the Holston River near Knoxville with his three sons and it was said that his influence extended far and wide. They established a Presbyterian Church and school in the area for not just the children of white settlers, but for the offspring of black slaves attached to the various estates. It was William's wish that the slave children should be taught to read and write as well as the whites and to understand the Presbyterian catechisms. William lived until he was 92 and a grandson, James Houston Gillespie, became a Presbyterian minister. This section of the family spelt their surname Gillespie and it was to become the form in the years that followed.

Agnus and Elizabeth, surviving daughters of James and Jennet Gillespy, married and remained in the Shenandoah Valley.

THE HENRYS

James and Mary Henry were 1730s immigrants from Ulster and after spending a few years in New Jersey, they settled in Augusta County in Virginia. The family lived near Spottswood and they worshipped in New

Providence Presbyterian Church, where various members were elders. The Henrys were renowned Indian fighters and played a leading part in the Revolutionary War.

THE JAMISONS (JAMESONS)

The Jamisons/Jamesons who settled in Pennsylvania in the mid-18th century were in large part Presbyterians, drawn from the province of Ulster. York County in Pennsylvania was a popular stopping-off point before the families headed westwards to Virginia and Kentucky.

An Ulster-born John Jameson and his wife Jane Erwin were residing at Staunton in Augusta County in 1745 and three Jamisons - John, Robert and Thomas - are listed as having fought at the Battle of Kings Mountain in 1780. Descendants of the original Jamisons (Jamesons) moved on to Tennessee, Kentucky, Missouri and Texas.

A recent survey carried out worldwide by the Jamison (Jameson) International Registry, revealed that in the United States there were 26,457 bearing that name, in Northern Ireland 1690, Canada 757, mainland Britain 697, Australia 313, and New Zealand 185.

THE KILGORES

Five Kilgore brothers - Robert, Charles, William, Hiram and James - emigrated from the north of Ireland about 1763 and settled in southwest Virginia at Nickelsville in Scott County. They built a fort known at Kilgore Fort and all took part in the Battle of Kings Mountain in October, 1780 as members of the Virginia Militia. Charles and Robert were wounded in the battle.

THE LEATHS

James Leath, the first of this pioneering Scots-Irish family, arrived in America in the 1720s and took the set route from Pennsylvania to Virginia. He settled lands east of the South Shenandoah River on Jeremy's Run in present-day Page County. Some of his land extended to Franklin County and Augusta County and fell to George and Ephriam Leath, the two sons.

Both George and Ephriam had moved to the Shenandoah Valley in the mid-1730s with their father and are recorded in 1736 as settlers liable for land grant. As the years progressed, they kept adding to their lands and by the end of the 18th century the family owned thousands of acres of Virginia territory.

Third generation Leaths were located in North Carolina and East Tennessee (Greene and Jefferson Counties) and Ann, daughter of George, married Alexander Mathews/Mathes, who was a founding elder of the Salem Presbyterian Church at Washington County, East Tennessee, and a close associate of the Rev. Samuel Doak, the pioneer preacher.

THE MATTHEWS

The Mathews family of seven brothers and three daughters - William, Richard, James, John, Sampson, George, Archer, Jane, Rachel and Elizabeth - came from the north of Ireland in 1737 with their parents John and Anne (Archer) Mathews and they settled in Augusta County, Virginia about 1739. Descendants were Governor John P. Mathews, of Oregon, and Governor George Mathews, of Georgia.

Alexander Mathews, from Ballynure in Co. Antrim, came with the family of the Rev. Samuel Doak to America in 1740, landing at New Castle, Delaware. They settled in Chester County, Pennsylvania, but later moved to Augusta County, Virginia. Alexander Mathews acquired a lot of land in the Shenandoah and as a magistrate was one of General George Washington's main backers for high political office.

The Mathews and the Doaks remained close friends in Augusta County, settling on adjoining lands and worshipping together as devout Presbyterians. Alexander Mathews had twelve sons and one daughter, with four of the sons - Alexander, George, Jeremiah and Allen - moving to Jonesboro, the oldest town in Tennessee, at the end of the Revolutionary War. Alexander had been a captain in the militia - his brothers also serving at various grades. This was a real pioneering journey by the Mathews brothers for Tennessee was still a wilderness then, inhabited by few white settlers and a dangerous terrain where the native American tribes lived in large numbers.

On the long trek, the brothers changed their surname to Mathes, very probably through a mispelling, and the name continues to this day in Tennessee. Alexander was a surveyor and civil engineer and acquired

950 acres of land in Washington County, beside the Limestone River where Davy Crockett's family lived. He was closely associated with the Salem Presbyterian Church and Washington College, both founded by his friend the Rev. Samuel Doak. It was on Mathews land that both buildings were erected and Alexander was a founding elder of the church. His descendants were to continue in this tradition and a son, civil magistrate Ebenezer, an elder for 40 years at Salem and a trustee of Washington College for 46 years. He left half of his 7,000-dollar estate (a fortune at that time!) to both institutions. Ebenezer was an uncompromising supporter of the Union cause in the Civil War and a memorial window in Salem Church bears the inscription - "The Lord loves a cheerful giver".

THE McCAMPBELLS/ANDERSONS

John McCampbell moved with his family of three sons and three daughters from Co. Londonderry in the north of Ireland to America in 1753 and they settled at Rockbridge County in Virginia. Another son, James, remained in Ireland for a period, but made it eventually to Virginia. He was married to Mary Shannon, whose father was Samuel Shannon, one of the heroic figures in the Siege of Londonderry in 1688-89.

The McCampbells and their connections, the Shannons, Andersons, Smiths, Caldwells and the Chambers distinguished themselves as soldiers (in the Revolutionary War), in the church, as lawyers and in civic life. The families moved to a settlement known as "Grassy Valley" in Knox County, close to present-day Knoxville in East Tennessee and in 1802, with the help of pioneering preacher, the Rev. Samuel Carrick, they established Washington Presbyterian Church.

The first minister was the Rev. Isaac Anderson, grandson of Isaac Anderson who was born in Co. Down in 1730 and who arrived in Knox County in 1801 with his son William, from Rockbridge County, Virginia. William Anderson had five sons - the Rev. Isaac; Robert, a judge; Samuel and William, both lawyers and James, a colonel in the militia. Rev. Isaac Anderson founded Maryville College.

Washington, named after General George Washington, became the church of many Knoxville Valley settlers and even though another congregation was formed nearby at Spring Place in 1842, it continued to prosper. Later in 1886 in the same area the Shannondale Presbyterian

Church came into existence and today all three congregations still co-exist.

THE McCUES

The Rev. John McCue was the most illustrious pioneer of this strong Covenanting family. His father John had emigrated from Ulster in the early 1730s and settled at Lancaster County, Pennsylvania before moving on to Nelson County, Virginia in 1737. John, the eldest son, studied at Washington College under the Rev. James Waddell, whom he succeeded as minister of Tinkling Spring Church at Augusta County in Virginia, which was formed by the Rev. John Craig.

He founded one of the first Presbyterian churches west of the Allegheny Mountains at Lewisburg, Greenbriar County, and in 1791, when minister of Staunton Church, took over the Tinkling Spring charge. John McCue married a daughter of James Allen, of Augusta County, and his family distinguished themselves in the church, civic life and in the military. A grandson was Judge John H. McCue, of Augusta County.

THE McILHANEYS / BOWENS

THE McIlhaney / Bowen link was a joining of the Scots-Irish and Welsh Quaker connections through the marriage of Ulster-born Lily McIlhaney to Welshman John Bowen.

The couple lived in Pennsylvania and Maryland before coming to the Valley of Virginia at Augusta County near the James River in the 1740s. A son, Moses, died in the French and Indian War in 1761 and other members of the family were to serve in the Revolutionary War, with son Rees, a Virginia militia lieutenant, being killed at the Battle of Kings Mountain. A brother, Charles, was a militia captain in the Kings Mountain battle. John and Lily Bowen had 12 children, seven sons and five daughters.

Lily McIlhaney, was the daughter of Ulster-Scots immigrants Henry and Jane McIlhaney, from Co. Antrim. Her father died when she was an infant and she and her brother Henry were taken to America by her mother, who married a Mr. Hunter and had a large family. Records claim that the McIlhaney / Hunters brought the first flax wheel to Pennsylvania. Lily, born about 1705, was 17 when she married John Bowen, who, when he died in 1761, his will included five horses, ten cattle, and fifteen hogs, as well as extensive lands. Lily died in 1780 in Washington County, Virginia.

The McIlhaney (McElhaney) family, descended from Lily's brother Henry, settled widely in the Shenandoah Valley, south west Virginia and East Tennessee and were extensive landowners and leaders in business, church and civic life.

The stories of how the Bowen / McIlhaney families coped on the Virginia and Tennessee frontier with attacks from hostile Indian tribes are legendary. The women were as fearless as the men in defending their fortified homesteads, with Levisa Smith Bowen, wife of Rees Bowen, showing remarkable heroinism during one particular Indian attack at Maiden Spring, Tazewell County, Virginia in 1776. With the men absent from the fort, Levisa shouldered the only gun left, while the other women wielded sticks which the Indians took for firearms. They held the situation until the men returned and their bravery saved an almost certain massacre.

Colonel John H. Bowen was a noted lawyer and representative in the American Congress from Tennessee and William Bowen Campbell was Governor of Tennessee from 1851 to 1853.

THE McNUTTS

George McNutt, from mid-Co. Antrim close to the present-day town of Ballymena in Ulster, led his family through the Valley of Virginia to become one of Tennessee's most illustrious citizens. He was a Revolutionary War patriot and one of the heroes of the Battle of Kings Mountain.

George McNutt was living in south-western Virginia in 1779 with his first wife (he was married three times), Isabella Callison McNutt. He was born in Ulster, about 1751 and had emigrated to Virginia as a boy. A kinsman, Alexander McNutt, had been given royal grants of land in Nova Scotia, with the understanding that he was to bring settlers into the province. He brought several shiploads of emigrants from Ulster, including some of his relatives. Not all of the McNutts liked Nova Scotia and seeking a warmer climate, they moved into south-western Virginia. Later on, two of them, George and his cousin Benjamin, settled in Knox County, Tennessee.

By 1785, George McNutt had left Virginia to become one of the first residents of the"Irish Bottom", a settlement south of the French Broad River in what became Jefferson County seven years later and part of Tennessee. His daughter, Jenny, was born at "Irish Bottom" - said to be the first white child born south of the French Broad.

After about two years, McNutt moved his family to a new home, floating his goods down the river to the forks and settling on the north side of the Holston, a few miles upstream from White's Fort at Knoxville. There he stayed until his death 36 years later.

George McNutt became a leading figure in the growing communities in which he lived, both above and below the forks of the French Broad and Holston Rivers. He was an elder at the Rev. Samuel Carrick's Lebanon Presbyterian Church and, later, was one of the original bench of elders (along with Knoxville founder, James White) at First Knoxville Presbyterian Church. When Knoxville was founded in 1791, McNutt was named a town commissioner, along with John Adair and Paul Cunningham. And when Knox County was established in 1792, Territorial Governor William Blount appointed McNutt a justice of the peace. With James White, McNutt took the oath of office from Territorial Judge David Campbell.

George McNutt and James White had close personal ties in yet another way. In the late 1790s, McNutt's oldest daughter, Isabella, married James White's son, Moses, thus joining the blood-lines of these pioneering families.

George McNutt's concern for education is reflected in the fact that he was appointed a trustee of three pioneering institutions. He was a charter trustee of Blount College and Hampden Sidney Academy at Knoxville and a trustee of Washington College in Washington County, Tennessee.

McNutt collected an unusually large personal library for his time. His reading interests ranged from Shakespeare's plays to Newton's scientific writings; but his principal intellectual diet was religious works. An inventory of his personal belongings included his library of 26 books and 27 pamphlets; a pair of spectacles; four waistcoats; four pair of pantaloons; two hats; and a walking stick. Among his books were a Bible and hymn book; the Westminster Confession of Faith; John Knox's Essays; the Shorter Catechism; Newton's Works; an arithmetic book; and a volume of Shakespeare's plays.

On January 5, 1823, George McNutt died, aged 72. He was buried on a hill near his Knox County home.

THE NEVINS

John Nevin, a Covenanter-style Presbyterian from North Antrim, was involved in the United Irishmen rebellion of 1798 and had to flee to America to escape the agents of the Crown.

Nevin lived at Kilmoyle, four miles north of Ballymoney on the road to Portrush in Co. Antrim. He went into hiding when the rebellion collapsed and report has it he was smuggled through the town of Coleraine in a barrel. He made it to Knoxville in East Tennessee and prospered as a merchant until his death in 1806.

THE RAMSEYS

William Ramsey from Larne in Co. Antrim was the first of this family to land in the Shenandoah Valley, about the 1740s. He had settled for a time in Buck County, Pennsylvania and procured a sizeable tract of land at Green Forest near to Lexington in Rockbridge County.

The Ramseys had lived in Ulster from the Scottish plantation of the Province in the 17th century, having come from the Argyllshire region of Scotland. The Green Forest estate was later divided among William's three sons - William II, Samuel and James, who became a doctor. Each of the sons fought on the Revolutionary War against the Colonial Government.

The Ramseys were closely associated with the Lyle family, who came to Timber Ridge, Rockbridge County from Raloo near Larne and there was a lot of inter-marrying between the connections. Jane Lyle was the wife of Dr. James Ramsey (born 1756, died 1815), who had his 9,000-acre farm at Big Calfpasture Valley in the centre of the Shenandoah. This land is still in the family name.

Dr. James Ramsey served in Captain Andrew Wagoner's company of the 12th Virginia Regiment in the Revolutionary War and for his services he was awarded 300 acres of land in Kentucky. He rode on horseback from Lexington to Kentucky to claim the land, remaining there long enough to sell it and return to Virginia to buy the 9,000 acres at Big

Calfpasture River in Augusta County. On the estate Dr. Ramsey built a brick colonial-style house "Locust Grove", a magnificent building for the period, containing some interesting features. On the inside of one of the doors is a large cross outlined with round-headed hand-wrought nails - this being the symbol of a Christian home. On another door hangs an old cowhide latchstring - the symbol of hospitality.

Dr. Ramsey served for 22 years on the board of directors of Washington College, which was earlier known as Liberty Hall, but is now Washington and Lee University. The doctor had three sons - John, William III and Samuel Lyle and two daughters Sarah and Janetta, both of whom married Presbyterian ministers. William Ramsey III built a farm home on lands adjacent to his father's estate.

William Ramsey II, the eldest son of the original pioneer, married Sarah Fulton and had one daughter, but he tragically died in a drowning accident on the James River. Samuel, the other brother, married Elizabeth Lyle and had eight children. He lived and is buried at Timber Ridge.

Ten grandsons of Dr. James Ramsey served in the Confederate Army during the American Civil War, with five losing their lives. Brothers Thomas Alexander and William Waters Ramsey, the sons of William III Ramsey, and brothers James, Henry Kerr and Alexander Brown Ramsey, the sons of Samuel Lyle Ramsey. Brothers John Odell, Brown Clayton, and Robert Yates Ramsey (sons of William III Ramsey) served with distinction in the Virginia forces, under General Thomas "Stonewall" Jackson, as did William Scott and Samuel Newell Ramsey (sons of Samuel Lyle Ramsey).

Descendants of the original pioneer William Ramsey and his three sons gave outstanding public service in the church, as doctors and teachers, in military roles, and in civic and political life in the Valley of Virginia. They were a Scots-Irish family who prospered through their deeply-held faith, educational prowess, leadership qualities and industrious character.

• Strong Calvinist William Ramsey, the original settler from Larne, very generously financially aided a young Scottish youth, Archibald Scott, to obtain a Presbyterian theological education in Virginia. Rev. Scott became the first pastor of Bethel Presbyterian Church in the Shenandoah Valley in 1779 and four generations of his family followed him into the ministry.

THE TATES

The Tates, another family of Covenanting stock, were noted for their piety, industry and public spirit - typical Scots-Irish settlers in the Shenandoah Valley. The family arrived in Augusta County in 1745 and four brothers - James, William, John and Robert - settled the lands. James was killed at the Battle of Guilford during the Revolutionary War and his great grandson, the Rev. John C. Tate was a Presbyterian minister in Kentucky. A son, by his second marriage was Colonel William P. Tate, an Augusta County militia officer.

John Tate represented Augusta County in the Virginian state legislature in 1798, while a descendant of William, Dr. Thomas Tate, was a Virginian state senator and head of the civil service bureau in Washington.

THE TELFORDS

This family of Scots-Irish Presbyterians appear in Valley of Virginia records as early as 1740 with the settlement of Hugh Telford at Falling Spring. Later, in 1753, a family group of Telfords came from Co. Tyrone in the north of Ireland and settled at Rockbridge County, not far from Lexington. This is verified on a Revolutionary War pension for Irish-born John Telford made in Blount County, East Tennessee in 1832.

In the Valley of Virginia in the 1750s six Telford brothers - Alexander, Robert, James, David, John and Jeremiah - lived and prospered as farmers and merchants. They were the sons of Alexander Telford Sen., from Co. Tyrone in Ulster. Alexander, Robert and David Telford were listed for service in the French and Indian Wars of 1756 and Jeremiah was a member of the Augusta County militia in 1770. Robert Telford, a son of Alexander, also served in this militia. Captain Alexander Telford, was killed at the Battle of Guilford Courthouse in North Carolina in March, 1781 while leading the Virginia militia.

THE WALLACES/WOODS

Peter Wallace, a lowland Scot, settled in Ulster at the end of the 17th century and married Elizabeth Woods in 1704. He died in 1724 at the age of 44, but later that year his widow emigrated to America with her six children, five sons and one daughter, thus an illustrious chapter on the American frontier began.

They travelled across the Atlantic with Elizabeth's four brothers - Michael, James, Andrew and William Woods - and their families, landing at New Castle, Delaware and settling at Lancaster County, Pennsylvania. In 1739, Elizabeth moved to the Valley of Virginia to be near her brother Michael and his family and her final settlement was in Rockbridge County.

Four of Elizabeth's family married their cousins on the Woods side, further blood bonding the connection. The Wallaces and the Woods were strong Presbyterians and William Wallace (Peter and Elizabeth's eldest son) and his father-in-law Michael Woods (Elizabeth's brother) were the principal founders of the Mountain Plains Church in Albemarle County in the Blue Ridge Mountains region. William and his wife Hannah had a plantation home at Greenwood, Piedmont and a descendant Hugh Campbell Wallace was a United States ambassador to France. Other descendants became prominent in Kentucky and Missouri.

Samuel Wallace, second son of Peter and Elizabeth, settled at Charlotte County in Virginia and he ended his days in Kentucky in 1800. A son Samuel headed for Scotland, very probably to check on his ancestral tree, and was never heard of again.

The third son Andrew, married his cousin Margaret, daughter of Michael Woods, in 1733 and they also lived at Albemarle County. The family spread out to Kentucky and Indiana and descendants included David Wallace, the Governor of Washington Territory, and General Lew Wallace (1827-1905), Governor of New Mexico territory and celebrated author of many books including Ben Hur, A Tale of the Christ, The Boyhood of Christ, and the Life of Benjamin Harrison. General Wallace fought in the Civil War and served on the court martial of Abraham Lincoln's assassin.

Susannah Wallace, the only daughter, married her cousin William Woods (son of Michael) and they also lived at Albemarle County. They had 12 children (seven sons and five daughters) and William inherited his father's plantation estate at Mountain Plains. In 1737, William received a land grant of 12,700 acres from the patronage of Sir William Gooch and in 1763 he gave half of the land to his son Adam. William, born at Castle Dunshanglin, Ireland in 1705, was a lieutenant, captain and colonel in the American militia.

Most of the family emigrated to Kentucky and Susannah is listed as an American Revolutionary War patriot (a distinction accorded to very few women) for the service she gave in providing military and food supplies to the forces on the front line. Her seven sons served as soldiers of rank in the Revolutionary War.

Peter Jun., the youngest child of Peter and Elizabeth Woods Wallace, married his cousin Martha Woods and they lived at Augusta County and Rockbridge County, close to Lexington. During the period 1750-1768, Peter acquired 500 acres of land, all near or bordering the James River, and in addition to his farming pursuits, he was also land appraiser for the region. Both he and his wife worked tirelessly for the Timber Ridge Presbyterian Church.

In 1775, the Wallaces and their relatives - the Woods, the McDowells, and the Lapsleys - took part in the rebellion against the Governor Lord Dunmore, who had tried to confiscate all the powder and war munitions that the Virginians had been collecting. Dunmore was forced to back down in the face of the determined frontiersmen, the Revolutionary War had started in earnest.

All six sons of Peter Jun. served as officers in the Revolutionary War, with Samuel a colonel in command at Fort Young on the Virginian border in the French and Indian War of the 1750s/60s. Four were killed in action and a fifth died shortly after the War. Members of the family made settlements in Tennessee, Kentucky and Indiana.

A great grandson of Peter Jun. was William Alexander Anderson Wallace, known as 'Big Foot' Wallace. A bronze statue stands in the centre of Lexington to the memory of this brave Shenandoah-born Texas Ranger, Indian fighter, and hunter bearing the inscription:

"Big Foot Wallace 1817-1899."

"William Alexander Wallace was born one mile south of this corner marker in a brick house still standing, which was near the dwelling of his grandfather Samuel Wallace, where the first Rockbridge Court was held in 1778. At the age of 23, he went to Texas to avenge the death of his brother, who was massacred by the Mexicans at Goliad. He served his adopted state as an Indian fighter, Ranger, Civil War soldier and post carrier, enduring great hardship and ordeals recorded in history. His remains are interred at San Antonio, and the state of Texas has signally honoured his memory. Wallace motto - Sperandum. Erected by his Virginia and Texas admirers. 1935."

THE WHITSITTS (WHITESIDES)

This Presbyterian family can be traced back to William Whitsitt, who emigrated to America from Ulster with his wife Elizabeth (Dawson) Whitsitt and their son William, about 1732. The Whitsitts landed in Pennsylvania with other kinsfolk who had come from Co. Antrim, Co. Armagh and Co. Tyrone where the family tended to be known more as Whitesides. William Whitsitt (or Whiteside) settled in Albemarle County, Virginia close to the Blue Ridge Mountains and farmed an extensive acreage of land.

The family were involved in the setting up of the Presbyterian Church at Ivy Creek and it was reported that the evangelist, the Rev. George Whitefield preached in William's tobacco barn. The Whitsitts (Whitesides) fought in both the French and Indian Wars of 1755-63 and in the Revolutionary War a decade and more later.

Some of the family moved on to Tennessee and it was the Nashville connection who gave acceptance to common usage of the surname Whitsitt. William always signed his name Whiteside and the name of his son was written Whiteside in the records of the Albemarle militia, but when he moved to Amherst County in another part of Virginia he began to call himself Whitsitt.

William Whitsitt's grandson, the Rev. James Whitsitt was a pioneering pastor of the Baptist church in Nashville, a Godly man who had been inspired by the Revivalist preaching of the Rev. George Whitefield.

• A family of Whitsitts were Quakers who belonged to the Grange Meeting House outside Dungannon in the early 1700s.

THE WILSONS

William Wilson and his wife, Barbara McKane, emigrated from the north of Ireland in 1729 to Pennsylvania where their six children were born. In 1747 they moved to Virginia, first to Augusta County and then to the Jackson River Valley. They settled on about 1,000 acres and William built a grist mill in 1753.

Because of incessant Indian raids, the Wilsons moved back to Augusta County in 1760, but three years later the attacks were renewed with fatalities. During one attack William was building a larger house and John, the older son, had gone to get nails when the Indian surprised the women by the river. A tomahawk hit the mother on an arm. Barbara, a daughter, was knocked down and never fully recovered from her injuries. Susan, another daughter, repelled one Indian from the cabin by smashing a hot iron on his hand. Thomas, another son, was captured and died in captivity. The attack deeply scarred the family.

John Wilson (1732-1820), William's son, served in the Augusta militia in the French / Indian War and was appointed major during the Revolutionary War. Upon the creation of Bath County in 1791, he was appointed one of the original justices. In 1786 John Wilson married Sarah Alexander, daughter of Robert Alexander and Esther Beard. They had three children - William, Esther and Margaret. This Robert Alexander started the first classical school in Augusta County, which became Liberty Hall and in turn was the forerunner of today's Washington and Lee University.

"We see many every day travelling to Carolina, some on foot with packs, and some in large covered wagons. The road here is much frequented."

- A Presbyterian minister in the Valley of Virginia in 1775, describing the westward migration.

"It is Scotch-Irish in substantial origin, in complexion and history - Scotch-Irish in the countenance of the living and the records of the dead."
-Report to the American Congress in the late 18th century about Western Pennsylvania and Pittsburg.

19

The pioneering *McReynolds from Co. Tyrone*

T he McReynolds of Virginia and East Tennessee were originally Scottish stock who became deeply rooted in the Killyman and Clonoe regions of Co Tyrone in the north of Ireland at the end of the 17th century. They were a typical pioneering family on the American frontier and their distinguished and daring exploits over several centuries have given them a special niche in the history of the United States.

John McReynolds (McRannells), an Episcopalian by religion, was born at Inverary in Scotland in 1672 and as a 16-year-old youth suffered great hardship inside the walls of Derry during the Siege of 1688/89. His grandson's diary recalls how he "gave someone a scrubbing for letting a rat escape that they were to eat for supper during the Siege". John sided with Protestant King William 111 who defeated the Roman Catholic King James 11 at the Battle of the Boyne. He married Mary Preston, daughter of a local Co. Tyrone farmer in 1703, and they lived at Cloghog near the town of Dungannon. The couple had three sons, but when Mary died in 1713, aged only 30, John married a Quaker girl Elizabeth Shepperd and joined Grange Meeting near Moy in Co. Tyrone.

John, a fluent speaker of the Scottish Gallic language, had accumulated much property, by the standards of the period, owning several farms and mills at Killyman and Clonoe. He was considered a man of real substance. His second wife was much younger than he and, when a decision was taken in 1737 for the family to emigrate to America, John, then a man of 72, opted to remain in Ireland with the children of the first marriage and their families. He returned to the Church of Ireland for it must have been difficult for a former mercenary soldier to adopt Quaker pacifist ideals. John died at the Kingsmills, Stewartstown, Co Tyrone home of a grandson, aged 95. He is buried in the Ballyclog Cemetery alongside other family members.

The single-storey thatched-roofed Kingsmills farmhouse at Stewartstown, built in 1747 by Dr. James McReynolds, remains in possession of the McReynolds family, who are still working the land in this western part of Ulster and are intensively proud of their historic ties with the American frontier states.

Elizabeth Shepperd McReynolds, John's wife, led her four young children from the marriage — Joseph, James, Robert and Elizabeth, daughter-in-law Sarah Dixon McReynolds (Joseph's wife), and several relatives, on the long journey to America and their first settlement was at Lancaster County in Pennsylvania. There, the sons became apprenticed to the carpentry trade and worked on the farmlands.

Various theories can be expounded as to why John McReynolds decided against joining his wife and children in the long trek to a new life in America. Age was definitely against him and he also had the children from the first marriage all around him. His wife's willingness to move was very probably motivated by the fact that she was a Quaker, or a member of the Society of Friends, a denomination which was subject to persecutions under the Test Act as much as Presbyterians and other nonconformist dissenters in the 18th century, in both England and Ireland. Elizabeth's brother Solomon and other Quaker relatives had already gone to America.

Persecution of the Quakers was rife and members of the Society were fleeing the British Isles in large numbers. The leading figure in the Quaker movement in the late 17th and early 18th centuries had been William Penn, the son of Admiral William Penn. King Charles 11 of England owed Penn's father a debt with interest amounting to about £80,000 and in 1680 Penn asked the King to pay the money to him in wilderness land in America instead. The King agreed to the request and Penn received the territory west of the Delaware River between New York and Maryland and power over the territories. The King asked Penn to name the colony after Penn's father and in this way Pennsylvania, which means Penn's Woods got its name. William Penn as a young man had joined the religious order known as Friends or Quakers and because of the religious persecutions he opened the Pennsylvania colony to any who wished to move there and establish a new life of peace and freedom. The only requirement was that they had to take up residence on the claim.

Joseph McReynolds, the eldest of John and Elizabeth's family, was a deeply religious man who embraced the Presbyterian faith with great fervour and both he and his brother James were greatly influenced by the 1749 George Whitefield-led revival in Pennsylvania. Like their mother, they had been Quakers in Ulster and for a time in America, they attended New Gordon Quaker meeting house a short distance away in Cecil County, Maryland, but James and Joseph were disjoined for consorting with Methodists and "New Light" Presbyterians. Joseph was baptized into the Presbyterian Church by Gilbert Tennant, whose pioneering father William Tennant had emigrated from Co. Armagh.

Joseph moved to Campbell County, Virginia and, after several years, to Washington County, Virginia, close to the Holston River. Around 1800 he settled with his son Samuel in the Sequatchie Valley of the Tennessee River at Bledsoe County in Tennessee and died in 1805, aged 90. He served in the Revolutionary War in Captain Harry Terrall's Company of the 5th Virginia Regiment. He and his wife Sarah had seven sons and two daughters.

One son Robert was ensign and recruiting officer in the 19th North Carolina Regiment. He had been born on the Atlantic Ocean on route to America in 1737 and his son Joseph was recruited into the Revolutionary War forces at the age of 16 and received a crippling ankle wound at the Battle of Camden in 1780.

A family record of the McReynolds move to America in 1737 relates how the journey across the Atlantic took six weeks to complete, having lost its way for a time. "Provisions became exhausted and the wanderers faced starvation. But fortunately, another ship appeared looking like a buzzard, as some passengers expressed it, and helped them complete their journey".

One of this line of the McReynolds family was James Beriah Frazier, who became Governor of Tennessee and was a United State Democratic Senator at the turn of this century. Two of his forebears were Samuel and Abner Frazier, who fought at the Battle of Kings Mountain.

James McReynolds (1719-1807) married Mary Bell, from a family of similar Ulster-Scots background. Mary's father Thomas had been a shoemaker in the Co Tyrone town of Omagh, 20 miles from Dungannon, and he was a pillar of the Presbyterian Church, both in his native home-land and in Maryland and Pennsylvania where he settled. Two years after they married, James and Mary Bell McReynolds left Pennsylvania for Virginia and they rented land at Little Roanoke River in Charlotte County. More land was acquired at Campbell County on Falling River and it was there that James finished his days. He was a very industrious man and had an excellent reputation in the region where he lived. When speaking of moral honesty, it was frequently said "as honest as James McReynolds". James, and son Thomas, played their part in the Revolutionary War with the Campbell County militia and his wife Mary was also cited as a patriot for her role in delivering supplies and ammunition to the front lines. They had nine sons and a daughter. Mary died in 1799, aged 70.

Robert McReynolds died of pleurasy soon after he had completed his carpenter's apprenticeship at Lancaster County, Pennsylvania. Elizabeth McReynolds, the daughter, married a Joseph Rodgers and after living in Maryland for a period moved back to Pennsylvania. They had four sons and a daughter and one of the sons William was massacred in an Indian raid. Descendants moved to Kentucky and Tennessee.

The McReynolds clan aligned themselves mainly with the Confederate cause during the American Civil War of 1861-65 and members of the family fought at different levels. Allen McReynolds, a wealthy Missouri businessman, born at Washington County, Virginia, was executed by the Union militia in 1864 for having fed and aided Quantrell's Confederate Raiders. McReynolds's prominence in Missouri prompted the Adjutant General of the United States Army to demand an investigation into the murder, but the atrocity was covered up as an episode of war.

Jacob McReynolds and his wife Anna Christina McReynolds made it to California in 1852, after a several thousand-mile trek from Washington County through Illinois, Missouri, and Oregon. It was a journey which took the most of 15 years as they settled in one place, and then moved on to another. The couple had a family of fifteen, eleven sons and four daughters, and it was three of the sons who suggested California as a place of settlement after being involved in the "Gold Rush of '49".

Two descendants of the pioneering McReynold's of the mid-18th century were prominent public figures during the Presidential period of Franklin Delano Roosevelt in the early part of this century. Samuel Davis

McReynolds was a strong supporter of Roosevelt and chairman of his Foreign Affairs Committee in Congress. James Clark McReynolds, an opponent of Roosevelt, was descended from James and Mary Bell McReynolds, while Samuel Davis McReynolds came from the Joseph and Sarah Dixon McReynolds line. James Clark McReynolds was born in 1862 in Elkton, Kentucky, close to the birthplace of both Abraham Lincoln and Jefferson Davis, the President of the Confederacy. His family was very influential in the politics of the day — a cousin was Benjamin H. Bristow, Secretary of the United States Treasury during Ulysses Grant's Presidency, and another cousin was Ninian Edwards, the first Governor of the State of Illinois and the first United States Senator from that state. James Clark was the son of Dr. John O. McReynolds of Middle Tennessee, and he was a science graduate from the Vanderbilt University in Nashville, finishing top in a class of 100.

McReynolds practised law in Nashville and taught at Vanderbilt University for several years. In 1896 he stood for Congress as a Gold Democrat, but was defeated. However, in 1903 he was appointed as Assistant Attorney General under Philander Knox by President Theodore Roosevelt and he continued in that post until 1907 during the administration of President William Howard Taft. He became Attorney General in 1913, at President Woodrow Wilson's invitation, and was an influential figure in this First World War administration.

In cabinet, James Clark McReynolds, a bachelor, proved difficult to deal with and he had a belligerant streak. He was said to be proud, sensitive, and aloof, the least popular of the Wilson administration, but the most inscrutable. In spite of his reputation as a radical, he was at heart an ultra-conservative who took a narrow view of the role government should play in economic affairs. Later, James Clark, out of Government but still a member of the Supreme Court, was a vitriolic opponent of the New Deal offered by Franklin D. Roosevelt in the post-Depression years of the 1930s.   James Clark McReynolds died in Washington in 1946, aged 84.

Samuel Davis McReynolds, a far distant cousin of James Clark McReynolds, was also a Tennessean, born in 1872 at Pikeville, son of a farming couple Isaac S. McReynolds and Virginia Adeline Davis McReynolds. He was a lawyer, who, after holding practices at Pikeville and Chattanooga, was appointed judge of the Criminal Court for the Tennessee Circuit in 1903, a position he held for 20 years. Known as

Sam to friends and supporters, McReynolds started his US House of Representatives career in 1923 as a conservative, but, under the New Deal policies, became an influential supporter of President Roosevelt. As leader of the House Foreign Affairs (Representatives) Committee, he advanced the power of the President and one of his favourite policies was co-operation with Great Britain in the Pacific region. He also fought strenuously for a geographical wage differential favouring Southern states. When he died in 1939, Sam McReynolds was paid this tribute by President Roosevelt — "As a national legislator Sam McReynolds brought to his public duties exceptional ability, integrity, and great capacity for work".

James Clark McReynolds and Samuel McReynolds were in the highest tradition of a people who made an indelible mark on the fabric of American life. Their roots had been forged 200 years earlier among the green bushes of Co Tyrone, where it is said that when John McReynolds first arrived the woods on the shores of Lough Neagh were so thick that it would have been possible to walk along their tops. These roots were taken across the Atlantic to be implanted on the American frontier by a strong-willed woman with idealistic Quaker ideals — Elizabeth Shepperd McReynolds.

• Hugh McReynolds (1750-97), born in Co Antrim and married to Elizabeth Snoddy, served in the Revolutionary War as a private from Pennsylvania. It is not known whether he was related to the McReynolds of Co Tyrone.

• Leading Bluegrass music performers Jim and Jesse McReynolds family are descended from the McReynolds family of Co. Tyrone who emigrated in 1737. Jim and Jesse, brought up in the coalmining region of Coeburn near Dungannon in the Clinch Mountain region of Virginia, were heirs to a family musical tradition. Their hillbilly style country and old-tyme gospel singing is complemented by the distinctive mandolin, banjo and fiddle backing from their Virginia Boys Band.

The McReynolds brothers have enjoyed a regular spot at the Grand Ole Orpy in Nashville for close on forty years, recorded a string of albums and toured all over the world. Jesse is renowned for his remarkable dexterity and speed on the mandolin - he invented a rolling, picking style similar to playing a banjo rather than a mandolin. Jim has a plaintive tenor voice, ideally suited for bluegrass music. They have performed several times at country music festivals in Northern Ireland and are deeply conscious of their Ulster family roots.

20

The Lyles *of Raloo and Timber Ridge*

M atthew Lyle who was born at Raloo near Larne in Co. Antrim was one of the founding fathers of Presbyterianism in the Valley of Virginia and along with brothers John and Daniel was instrumental in pushing the frontier on from the Shenandoah region.

When the Rev. John Blair, of the Presbytery of Donegal in Pennsylvania, visited Timber Ridge in Augusta County, Virginia (now Rockbridge County) in 1746 he "set in order" a church and Matthew Lyle was one of the first elders. The Scots-Irish settlers had been worshipping for five years at a meeting house in Timber Grove, but until the Rev. Blair's arrival they had not been organised as a church.

The formation of a proper church caused a split among some of the families and a new meeting house was erected on Matthew Lyle's land, with its certification for worship granted on May 20, 1748.

Matthew Lyle, born in 1711, married Esther Blair in 1731 and had lived on their Raloo homestead until 1737, when the lease from the Chichester landlords expired. When he was outbid for the lease and left homeless Matthew and his wife faced a crisis and it was then that they first considered emigrating to America. Word had reached that part of Ulster that land opportunities were being opened up on the Virginia frontier and it was known that Ephriam McDowell and his family, from the same locality, had gone in that direction and prospered. With no real home of their own, the decision of the Lyles to move was inevitable.

About 1740, Matthew and Esther embarked on the journey across the Atlantic, accompanied by their two young sons James (aged eight) and John (aged six). Daughter Elizabeth, then only five, was left at home with her grandparents the Blairs, probably because she had been willed lease of land from an uncle Daniel Blair.

Two other Lyle children, William and Robert, died in childhood, and another daughter Martha was born as the couple were in the course of their journey to America. The family arrived in Pennsylvania and moved to Augusta County, Virginia and the first record of Matthew Lyle in his new home is his signature on a petition, dated July 30, 1742, which was sent to Virginia Governor William Gooch, by 50 settlers requesting the appointment and commissioning of John McDowell as their captain for the defence of the frontier against raids by native Indian tribes.

Within a short period of time, Matthew Lyle acquired extensive lands and by 1755 this had totalled 751 acres. In 1746 he had purchased 451 acres from landowner Benjamin Borden at a cost of thirteen pounds and ten shillings. Seventeen years later he sold this property to his son John for five shillings, a token amount. When he made his will, on June 15, 1773, Matthew Lyle bequeathed the homeplace of 300 acres to his son James and another tract of 110 acres to his daughter Elizabeth, who was still back home in Ireland. This stipulated: "In case my daughter Elizabeth does not come in from Ireland within the term of three years this tract was to be the property of James, who was to pay his sister fifteen pounds current money."

Matthew died in April, 1774 at the age of 63, having been predeceased by his wife Esther some years before. They are both buried in the old Timber Ridge cemetery, in unmarked graves.

James Lyle, born in Ireland in 1732, grew into manhood on the frontier and received a good education, at the school of Robert Alexander and the Rev. John Brown. He married Hannah Alexander, daughter of Archibald Alexander and Margaret Parks, who were married in Co. Antrim before they migrated to Nottingham in Pennsylvania and moved on to Virginia. James and Hannah had seven children: Joseph, Matthew, Elizabeth, Esther, Margaret, John and Archibald.

When he died in 1791, James Lyle owned not only the family homeplace, but 400 acres at Lick Creek in North Carolina; 500 acres " on the waters of Licking" in Kentucky and an interest, with Colonel

Samuel McDowell, in 1,000 acres in Kentucky. Eldest son Joseph served in the Revolutionary War, Matthew became a Presbyterian minister, John became a doctor and went to Florida and Archibald, who never married, fought with Andrew Jackson during the Indian War of 1812 and raised, organised and commanded a company of cavalry.

John Lyle, the other son of Matthew and Esther Blair Lyle, married Isabella Paxton, daughter of another Ulster-Scots couple John Paxton and his wife Mary Blair, about 1760. They spent most of their lives on the farm at Timber Ridge, and John was a militia captain in the Revolutionary War and participated in the expedition against the Cherokees under Colonel William Christian. They had three children: John, Esther and Mary Paxton.

Isabella Paxton Lyle died in 1780 and within a short time John married Frances Stuart, the daughter of Major Alexander Stuart and granddaughter of Archibald Stuart, who had moved from Ulster to Virginia in 1738. John, at the time of his second marriage, sold 351 acres of land at Timber Ridge to Alexander Campbell, receiving 12,000 pounds of "current money of Virginia" and he deeded 100 acres to a friend. Thus having disposed of his property left to him by his father, he moved on to Kentucky with wife Frances and two children from that marriage. - Alexander and Isabella.

John Jun. served in the Revolutionary War and received bounty lands in Kentucky; Esther married back into the Paxton connection and Mary Paxton married James McDowell, second son of Judge Samuel McDowell and his wife Mary McClung. James McDowell was a Revolutionary soldier and returned from Yorktown as an ensign. He and Mary Paxton also moved to Kentucky.

Elizabeth, the daughter of Matthew Lyle who remained behind at Raloo, married William Thompson when she was 16 and after nine years of the marriage she was left a widow with three young children - Esther, Jane and Mary. She married Matthew Donald about 1765 and a year after her father died in 1774 she moved to America to take up the 110 acres of land at Timber Ridge bequeathed to her in his will.

She died in 1802; her husband Matthew Donald 10 years later and they had seven children, one of whom, Matthew, became a Presbyterian minister. Elizabeth's three daughters from her first marriage had also settled in Virginia, but later moved with their own families to East Tennessee.

Martha, the fourth child of Matthew Lyle, married Matthew Houston, son of John Houston and she became an aunt of legendary General Sam Houston. Martha and her husband and seven children moved to Blount County in East Tennessee in 1790, settling beside the French Broad River.

John Lyle, the younger brother of Matthew Lyle by nine years, was also born on the old homestead at Raloo and he married Jean Owens from the nearby townland of Ballysnodd. They emigrated to America about 1745 and it is recorded that John Lyle purchased 734 acres of land at Mill Creek on Timber Ridge on March 19, 1746, from the heirs of Benjamin Borden, for twenty two pounds and five shillings current money. The land was close to that of Matthew Lyle and John McDowell, but sadly John passed away in 1758 at the age of only 38, although his wife lived for a further 49 years.

John was one of those who signed the call for the pastoral services of the Rev. John Brown at Timber Ridge Presbyterian Church and he contributed generously to the minister's stipend. He was also one of four bondsmen - John Berrisford, Robert Houston and Daniel Lyle (his brother) were the others - for the £150 required to build Timber Ridge Stone Church. John was an elder at the church for most of the time he lived in Virginia. His son John, also a Godly man, followed in the path of eldership at the church.

Daniel Lyle, brother of Matthew and John, also made it from Timber Ridge from Raloo and not only did he farm, but was a highly skilled stone mason who was in great demand for the construction of stone houses on the frontier. In 1756, he was one of the craftsmen employed in the construction of the old stone church at Timber Ridge and was also an elder in the congregation.

His wife was of the Paxton family, who had settled in Virginia after moving from Ulster through Pennsylvania. They had six children, five sons and a daughter - the eldest James, born in1751, was known as "red-headed Jimmy". It was said he was "a great stout fellow who could cut and maul two hundred rails a day". He married his cousin Sarah Lyle, daughter of his uncle John, the emigrant.

Another son Samuel was a weaver by trade, but when the Revolutionary War broke out, he served in the militia under Colonel William Christian in the expedition against the Cherokees. He fought at the Battle of Eutaw Springs in September, 1781 and was wounded in the leg. Samuel moved to Jefferson County in Tennessee and in 1784 married

Elizabeth L. White, a cousin of the Hon. Hugh L. White, a Tennessee Congressman for many years and a nominee for the American Presidency in 1836. When Tennessee was organised as a state in 1796, Samuel Lyle was elected Registrar of Jefferson County and held the position until his death in 1834. John, the youngest son of Daniel Lyle, fought in the Battle of Point Pleasant in 1774 and after study at the Rev. Samuel Doak's Washington College, became a Presbyterian minister and carried on a ministry at Georgetown in Kentucky.

The Lyle brothers of Raloo made an outstanding contribution to the creation of orderly civilised life in the Valley of Virginia in the mid-18th century and their offspring carved an indelible stamp on the frontier as it moved westward.

★★★

Co. Down brothers Robert and James Maxwell took part in the infamous Boston Tea Party in 1773 dressed as Indians. The Scots-Irish Maxwells were part of a radical group called 'The Sons of Liberty' campaigning for American independence.

★★★

"It looks as if Ireland were to send all her inhabitants. If they continue to come they will make themselves proprietors of the Province. Last week there were no less than six ships and every two or three" - the words of James Logan, Governor of Pennsylvania, in 1725. Logan, an Ulster Quaker from Lurgan in Co. Armagh, was Provincial Secretary, Chief Justice of the Supreme Court and Mayor of Philadelphia.

21

Belfast News Letter *records the movement to America*

The first newspaper to publish the full text of the Declaration of Independence outside America was the Belfast News Letter, Northern Ireland's leading morning newspaper and of which the author of this book is assistant editor. Details of the Declaration had arrived by ship from America in the port of Londonderry about six weeks after it was signed and it was taken 100 miles to the offices of the Belfast News Letter, then published by brothers Henry and Robert Joy.

The news caused much stir in Belfast and for the News Letter, which also carries the distinction of today being the oldest newspaper in the English-speaking world, founded in 1737, it was a European scoop. King George III in London had not even been acquainted of the news of the Declaration - News Letter readers in Belfast were among the first to know on their side of the Atlantic. Later in its edition of September 6-10, 1776, the News Letter reported on the historic events in Philadelphia.

"The 4th of July, 1776, the Americans appointed as a day of fasting and prayer, preparatory to their dedicating their country to God, which was done in the following manner: 'The Congress being assembled after having declared America independent, they had a crown placed on a Bible, which by prayer solemn devotion they offered to God. The religious ceremony being ended they divided the crown into 13 parts, each of the United Provinces taking a part'."

The News Letter had been an influential vehicle for relaying news of the migration of the Scots-Irish Presbyterians to America. The paper carried many advertisements for the passage to America, most of them making special provision for contracted labour in the new lands.

Conscious of the strong link between Ulster and the American colonies the News Letter kept its readers fully informed about developments affecting their kinsfolk across the Atlantic. The events leading up to and during the War of Independence were fully detailed and news of the crucial Battle of Kings Mountain in South Carolina on October 7, 1780 was reported in the Belfast News Letter issue of February 6, 1781.

The Belfast News Letter, together with the Londonderry Journal, provided a full list, times and fares of the emigrant ships which sailed to America from the Ulster ports of Belfast, Londonderry, Larne, Portrush and Newry. The News Letter's policy at the time was against emigration, which they maintained robbed the north of Ireland of some of its finest and most industrious citizens, but this did not prevent the newspaper from carrying the advertisements for the ships.

In 1773 the News Letter reported that the emigrants were each paying three pounds, five shillings for their full passage across the Atlantic. The increased flow of people ensured that the ship owners were able to reduce the fare, because 50 years earlier when the trade was just opening up it was costing £7 to £9 to make the journey.

These fares have to set against the fact that the annual wage for an Irish labourer then was only £10 and those seeking to emigrate, but who had not the money to pay for their passage, travelled as indentures. By this method they agreed to work on board the ship and for a period when they arrived on American soil.

Of the almost 500 ships which advertised sailing from Ulster ports in the period 1750-1775, one third left Belfast; 30 per cent Londonderry; 19 per cent Newry; 13 per cent Larne and seven per cent Portrush. The ship owners had agents based in almost every main town in the north of Ireland and one of the key players in linking up the Ulster/American movement was Alexander McNutt, a native of Londonderry who emigrated to America in 1750 and settled for a time at Staunton, Virginia.

McNutt, a man of boundless energy and dauntless persistence, worked closely with the government in London on land promotion in the American colonies and in the Canadian settlement of Nova Scotia and he was responsible for the movement of tens of thousands of Ulster people. He hired ships and commandeered crew at the various ports and saw to it that lands were available when the emigrants arrived in America.

His contemporaries in North American land promotion in the 18th century were Arthur Dobbs, a large Carrickfergus, Co. Antrim land-owner of aristocratic background who concentrated in North Carolina; Thomas Desbrisay, a soldier-cum-land-promoter who moved emigrants to the Canadian settlements and Matthew Rea, a man of more lowly stature from the Co. Down village of Drumbo, but one with enough wit and intelligence to act as a successful middle man in the business of transporting people to the New World. Rea moved large numbers of Co. Down and Co. Antrim people to Georgia and the Carolinas.

The six-week journey to America was a hellish two months that brought those making the trip close to death with disease and pestilence, shortages of water and food and the brutalities of ship masters and crew. Piracy was another danger they faced on the high seas and many perished before they could come in sight of American land.

Overcrowding on the ships was a common feature, but generally, although provisions like meat and bread were not extended to the passengers in plentiful supply, the majority of the immigrants survived the journey. They may have arrived on the American shoreline badly in need of nourishment, but their hopes were raised by the sight of the new land and the prospect of a new life.

"My Ulster blood is my most precious heritage"

- the words of American President James Buchanan, whose family left Deroran near Omagh, Co. Tyrone and Co. Donegal in 1783, eight years before he was born in Pennsylvania in 1791.

"No country gave us so many of our inhabitants as Ireland."
                              - Dr David Ramsey, historian of South Carolina.

"Our prosperity is largely due to the Ulster people and their descendants and, from them, the blood was scattered throughout the south and the south western states."
                              - Governor Gilmer, historian of Georgia.

22

Staunton's link *with the Scots-Irish pioneers*

A simple thatched farmhouse from Co. Tyrone nestles snugly in the Shenandoah Valley overlooking the beautiful Blue Ridge Mountains of Virginia. Its prime spot location at the Museum of American Frontier Culture at Staunton has particular significance. The 18th century single-storey cottage provides an illuminating insight into the humble mode of life for the hardy Ulster-Scots Presbyterian settlers who left the north of Ireland to settle on the Appalachian frontier 200/250 years ago.

The cottage, in the traditional architectural form of homesteads that were dominant in the Ulster of the 18th and early 19th centuries, was originally in place at Claraghmore near Drumquin in Co. Tyrone. It was removed stone by stone, shipped across the Atlantic and is now deeply rooted in American soil and the subject of much interest for many of the 100,000 people who flock to the Staunton-based museum every year.

Staunton, population 25,000 and like the city of Rome bounded by seven hills, is a go-ahead prosperous town right in the heart of the Shenandoah Valley. There are more Stauntonites with Ulster-Scots blood in their veins than the descendants of any other ethnic group, and they are people of standing and real influence in the town.

The mission of the Museum of Frontier Culture is to increase understanding of those cultures which sent significant numbers of 18th century immigrants to the back-country of the Upper South and Middle Atlantic region of the United States. "We seek to promote the American culture that results from the interaction of the European settlers who came to this region between 1730 and 1840, and who contributed to the westward expansion of the American nation beyond Virginia", says Judge George M. Cochran, chairman of the Museum of American Frontier Culture in Staunton

The Ulster-Scots tradition is one of these cultures and in the Shenandoah Valley of Virginia from the 1730s on when the first settlers came pouring in from Pennsylvania it became a dominant strain alongside that of the Germans and the English. The Museum collects and preserves buildings, artifacts and research materials that illustrate the life and work of the pioneering Scots-Irish, German and English and over the past decade close ties have been established with the Ulster American Folk Park at Camphill near Omagh in Co. Tyrone.

The Ulster section at the Staunton museum is authentic right down to the neat drills of potatoes, turnips and cabbage in the fields surrounding the whitewashed cottage and the linen weaving looms that produced the fabric which was an economic lifeline for people back in the 18th century. Virginia has a hotter, drier climate than Ireland, but workers at the Ulster farm in Staunton have still managed to create an environment that closely resembles the landscape of the old country.

The farm complex has three buildings: basic living quarters with a byre annex, a pig craw/henhouse with dovecote in the gable, and a long outshed containing the turf store, cart shed and a cow byre. All are built of double sandstone walls with the cavity filled with rubble. The roofs are thatched with rye straw held in place by wooden pins called scollops.

Close by is a blacksmiths' forge, moved to the Staunton site from the townland of Keenaghan in Co. Fermanagh, where four generations of one family made and repaired simple tools or domestic ironware and shod animals for their neighbours. Again the stone construction and thatch roof of the forge are typical of 18th century Ulster and the centrepiece is a raised hearth backed by frame-mounted bellows.

For the Scots-Irish farm, staff from the Museum of Frontier Culture and the Ulster American Folk Park at Omagh, researched and prepared landscape plans to reflect the original concept back in the north of Ireland. The road in front of the cottage follows the old road bed, and white hawthorn hedgerows and stone walls enclose the fields.

Occupying similar space on the 80-acre Staunton site are American, German and English farms and a Valley of Virginia barn, which would have been typical of a Shenandoah Valley home of the mid-18th century.

23

Tracing the roots *back to Ulster*

Nowhere is the story of the Ulster emigrants to American over several centuries told more vividly than at the extensive outdoor museum at Camphill near Omagh in Co. Tyrone. The Ulster-American Folk Park, in its authentic rural setting in the foothills of the Sperrin Mountains, accurately portrays what life was like, both at home in Ireland and in America, for the families who moved to the New World in the 18th and 19th centuries.

The Folk Park, founded in 1976, as part of the American bicentennial celebrations, incorporates the ancestral cottage of Thomas Mellon, who as a boy of five left Castletown for America in 1818 and subsequently formed a vast industrial and commercial empire. It includes, in addition to the Mellon farmstead, a replica of the thatched Presbyterian meeting house where young Thomas Mellon worshipped, the local school (transported from its original 18th century site), a weaver's cottage, as weaving was a feature of life in the West Tyrone countryside, and a blacksmith's shop.

Thomas Mellon was descended from Archibald Mellon and his wife Elizabeth, lowland Scottish Presbyterians, who arrived in Ulster in 1660 and settled on a farm near the town of Omagh in Co. Tyrone.

A permanent exhibition at the Folk Park 'Emigrants' tells the story of over two centuries of emigration to America. The exhibition is divided into four principal sections: People and Places - the people who emigrated and their places of origin. Failure and Opportunities - the reasons for emigration. Transport and Migration - the emigration process including routes, ports and ships. Survival and Prosperity - settlement in the New World.

Representing the second or 19th century emigration is the thatched cottage which was the boyhood home of Archbishop John Hughes who built St. Patrick's Roman Catholic Cathedral in New York. Archbishop Hughes was born only a few miles from Castletown, and was closely associated with the great 19th century waves of Irish Roman Catholic immigrants entering America through New York. In the old world side is the home of Hugh and Robert Campbell. This two-storey dwelling, originally located at Aghalane townland near Plumbridge, dates from 1768. Hugh and Robert emigrated to America in 1818 and became successful merchants. The interior of the house has been restored to illustrate the living conditions of a prosperous Ulster family at the beginning of the 19th century.

Also on site is the original Mountjoy Post Office, Co. Tyrone which complements a 19th century Ulster street and gallery area, complete with dockside buildings and emigrant ship. Lying in the dock is a reconstruction of an early 19th century 'brig' modelled on the brig Union which carried members of the Mellon family to Baltimore in 1818. The dockside buildings, still retaining their original features, have been moved in brick by brick and re-built. A dockside building from Great George's Street in Belfast has been furnished as a merchant's office, and an 18th century house from Bridge Street in Londonderry represents the type of boarding accommodation where Thomas Mellon recalled having spent several weeks before setting out on the long sea voyage. In the 'New World' section there is a replica of the first log cabin, home of the Mellon family and of the two storey hewn-log house and its barn they built as their farm prospered.

Between 1700 and 1900 an estimated two million people left Ulster in search of a better life in America and Canada.

• People and Places - encapsulates the experiences of many thousands of emigrants by detailing the lives and experiences of a few; men such as John Dunlap - most famous as the printer of the American Declaration of Independence.. Thomas Mellon - who left Co. Tyrone in 1818 and founded one of the greatest financial dynasties in America - the Mellon Bank.

• Failure and Opportunity - why did so many people leave? This section of 'Emigrants' offers some answers. The impact of population growth in the 18th and 19th centuries is an important factor allied to on-going social, religious and economic tensions. Crop failures, economic depression and a desire in the hearts of many to own their own land led thousands upon thousands to risk the unknown to seek a better life in America. In the mid-19th century perhaps the greatest stimulus to emigration was the Great Famine of 1845-49, which forced in excess of one million people to leave Ireland, never to return.

• Transport and Migration - the 3,000-mile crossing of the Atlantic in the 18th and 19th century represented a traumatic obstacle. Many who decided to emigrate would rarely have ventured outside their own locality; and one can only attempt to imagine their feelings of fear and heartbreak as they boarded the small sailing ships in Belfast, Newry or Londonderry. For many the Atlantic crossing was just the beginning of an epic journey and this section of 'Emigrants' also deals with how the American frontier was rolled back.

• Survival and Prosperity - many people arrived in America with little except the clothes on their backs - 'Emigrants' graphically illustrates their struggle to survive in a new land and how they adapted their skills to overcome the difficulties of life in the American backcountry and the ever increasing urban sprawls of the 19th century. For many these early years were a battle to survive but they were motivated by a desire to make a new life, a dream which they could perhaps never have attained in Ireland.

The Ulster-American Folk Park is twinned with the Museum of American Frontier Culture at Staunton, Virginia, both fulfilling a role in preserving and enhancing the cultural and historical traditions of the emigrants, in their homelands and in their new settings.

In 1995 137,440 people visited the Folk Park at Castletown, an increase of 20,359 on the figure for 1994. A great many of these visitors were Americans seeking information on their family roots with the north of Ireland.

★★★

Hi! Uncle Sam!
    When freedom was denied you,
And Imperial might defied you,
    Who was it stood beside you
At Quebec and Brandywine?
    And dared retreats and dangers,
Redcoats and Hessian strangers,
    In the lean, long-rifled Rangers,
And the Pennsylvania Line!

Hi! Uncle Sam!
    Wherever there was fighting,
Or wrong that needed righting,
    An Ulsterman was sighting
His Kentucky gun with care:
    All the road to Yorktown,
From Lexington to Yorktown,
    From Valley Forge to Yorktown,
That Ulsterman was there!

Hi! Uncle Sam!
    Virginia sent her brave men,
The North paraded grave men,
    That they might not be slave men,
But ponder this with calm:
    The first to face the Tory,
And the first to lift Old Glory
    Made your war an Ulster story:
Think it over, Uncle Sam!

W. F. Marshall (Rev),
        Co. Tyrone

★★★

24

Tradition of *moonshining in Virginia*

Mention white lightning to the folks in the Appalachian mountain region of America and you can be sure they will not at all confuse it with the electric magnetisms that frequently occur in the skies. White lightning is the term used in the Appalachians to describe moonshine or illicit spirit, and if you know the right people you can be pointed in the direction of a still.

A tipple of moonshine can easily be obtained from folk in the Shenandoah Valley or in the region of western Virginia towards the state borders with Tennessee, North Carolina and Kentucky, where it is also in ready supply.

Making corn whiskey has been an important source of income in the Appalachian mountains since the first settlements in the 18th century and it was the Scots-Irish who are credited with bringing the practice to the American frontier from their former homelands.

The first settlers found the corn crop heavy and bulky to transport across the frontier regions to main market towns, but, by distilling the crop into whiskey, they found it less difficult to handle and there was invariably more revenue to be gleaned from the liquid assets than from the grain or meal.

Before they left Scotland and Ulster, the Scots-Irish settlers were forced to hide their small stills in wild and inaccessible places to avoid the British tax collectors. When the practice was introduced in America there were no federal authorities to contend with and during the Revolutionary War the Scots-Irish battalions were highly popular for the potent home brew they could instantly produce.

General George Washington, who enjoyed a tipple, was among their admirers, not just for their ferocity of the Scots-Irish in battle, but for their home brew. However, it was his Government which brought in a whiskey tax in 1791. This not only pushed the distillers underground, but provoked a bitter revolt by the small frontier farmers in the Appalachian states, many of them Scots-Irish, who had taken such a leading part in the Revolutionary War.

It was the feeling at the time that the distillation of the mountain spirit was a man's own business. He tilled the soil and grew his grain, so why should he have to pay a tariff on the whiskey he made on his own land?

Even now the "whiskey rebellion" is maintained in some quarters of the southern states. The moonshine tradition may still be illegal and the federal Government authorities may mount around-the-clock operations in a bid to catch the culprits, but to many inhabitants in the foothills of the Blue Ridge Mountains, the Smokies and the Alleghenies it is a perfectly normal cottage industry that fulfils a demand that is as insatiable today as it was for their hardy forebears 200/250 years ago.

The poteen practice is still exercised in a few remote areas of Northern Ireland and Scotland and there it is also illegal, with police, customs and the courts moving heavily in on those engaged in the undercover operations.

Moonshining in southern American states in the 1990s requires expensive apparatus, a considerable time factor, distilling skills and the nerve to risk jail or a heavy fine if caught in the act. For all the hazards, however, the Appalachian moonshiners carry on regardless and it is generally believed that if the practice was made a hanging offence, there would still be people prepared to take a chance. Appalachian moonshine is made from a variety of ingredients: barley, raisins, grapes, dandelions, rye, corn, peaches, apples, plums, persimmons, and tomatoes.

One of the most popular moonshine brews is "holiday whiskey", reserved for special days of the year. Brandy, made from apples or peaches, is also produced for Christmas and the New Year, selling at about 150 dollars a gallon. It is also common to have moonshine, known colloquially in Appalachia as white lightning, poured into a container of ice cream or added to the ingredients of a Christmas or Thanksgiving cake. The really cheap moonshine is a form of sugar liquid which is mixed either with peaches, plums or fox grapes.

There is also "coffee lace", the drink fermented by tipping a portion of moonshine into a cup of coffee. This has its origins in Irish coffee, but in places like Virginia it is served without the whipped cream and the foams. Making whiskey by the submarine method, a metal combustive container sited almost underground and capable of holding up to 600 gallons, is still in vogue. But wood fires are now seldom used to heat the liquor - bottle gas is a more effective and unobtrusive means of firing the spirits.

The moonshine industry operates by bush telegraph - you have got to know someone, who knows someone, to obtain supplies and this is usually found in remote, out-of-the-way places. The clear white spirit may not be displayed openly on the shelves of the local store, but it is readily available to those in positions of power, at county and state level.

"You don't go to a political rally in this area where there is whiskey served that you don't find a jar of clear whiskey sitting there", confirms one well-informed moonshine observer in Franklin County, western Virginia, a region heavily settled by Scots-Irish families two centuries ago.

During my visit to Western Virginia, I was offered a large sweetie-type jar of the white spirit, full proof I was assured, and not wanting to be discourteous to my genial welcoming host, and in the interests of research, I accepted this hospitality. However, there was no way I was going to injure my health or my reputation as an upstanding Ulster Presbyterian by drinking the stuff, or even risk prosecution by trying to take the moonshine home, through three airports. So I gladly parted the spirit to a Shenandoah worthy, who, with an inviting glint in his eye, said the stuff would come in useful as ingredient for a Christmas cake, or for medicinal purposes. He was very convincing and appreciative.

An Appalachian moonshiner can be an extremely God-fearing type who never misses Sunday worship at the local church. To some this contradiction can be explained thus: "Making whiskey and going to church are two different things. Whiskey is a living, going to church is your religion. It may not sit easily, but when the collection plate goes around at the service, the money from the moonshine man goes in with the rest".

Letter *from the President*

THE WHITE HOUSE

WASHINGTON

January 10, 1996

Mr. Billy Kennedy
c/o Causeway Press
9, Ebrington Terrace
Londonderry BT5 1JS
UNITED KINGDOM OF GREAT BRITAIN
    AND NORTHERN IRELAND

Dear Billy:

    I had a wonderful time during my visit to Northern Ireland and was delighted with the warm welcome I received. Mrs. Clinton joins me in thanking you for the copy of <u>The Scots-Irish in the Hills of Tennessee</u>. Your generosity made our trip especially memorable. We appreciate your thoughtfulness and send our best wishes.

Sincerely,

Bill Clinton

25

Pioneering *in the Smokies*

L amar Alexander, former Governor of Tennessee and a candidate for the Republican nomination in the 1996 American Presidential election, is intensely proud of his Scotch-Irish roots.

His Alexander and Rankin ancestors settled at Dumplin Valley in Jefferson County, East Tennessee in 1783 and worshipped at Mount Horeb Presbyterian Church. They had come from Londonderry, where members of the family had fought in the Siege of Londonderry in 1688 on the Protestant Williamite side and reached Tennessee via the Valley of Virginia.

Lamar Alexander tells of of his grandfather having a farm near Cassville in South West Missouri, which had been settled by the Rankins and Alexanders in the 1840s. He recalls: "These were descendants and the same wild and ornery Scotch-Irish frontiersmen - the Rankins, and the Alexanders - who pioneered Tennessee, fought hand-to-hand with the Cherokees for 30 years, and then moved west, looking for more fights."

• Lamar Alexander is from Blount County in East Tennessee, right in the heart of the Great Smoky Mountains, a region very heavily populated by Scots-Irish settlers and where General Sam Houston lived for a time. Lamar is deeply ingrained in the culture of East Tennessee and occasionally plays piano at country music jamborees.

They were Twain when they crossed the sea,
  And often their folk had warred;
But side by side, on the ramparts wide,
  They cheered as the gates were barred
And they cheered as they passed their King
  To the ford that daunted none,
For field or wall, it was each for all
  When the Lord had made them One.

Thistle and Rose, they twined them close
  When their fathers crossed the sea,
And they dyed them red, the live and the dead,
  Where the blue starred-lint grows free;
Here in the Northern sun,
Till His way was plain, He led the Twain,
  And He forged them into One.

They were One when they crossed the sea
  To the land of hope and dream.
Salute them now, whom none could cow,
  Nor hold in light esteem!
Whose footsteps far in peace and war
  Still sought the setting sun!
With a dauntless word and a long bright sword -
  The Twain whom God made One!

W. F. Marshall (Rev.)
Co. Tyrone

26

An American view *of the Scots-Irish*

T he term Scotch-Irish, is misleading in that it does not mean a mixture of two bloods but it is a term used for the lowland Scots who settled in the north of Ireland and their descendants. There was no blending of the two races. There was actually a law forbidding any Scotch settler or his children marrying any of the tribes or sects that made up the native race of Ireland.

The Scotch-Irish were a restless, hardworking and thrifty people. It was said that a "Scot-Irishman" is one who keeps the commandments of God and every other good thing he can get his hands on. They were a brave but hot-headed folk. They were quick tempered, rather visionary, imperious, and aggressive. They were clanish, contentious, and hard to get along with which is illustrated by this prayer attributed to them:

"Lord grant that I may always be right, for thou knowest I am hard to turn".

The Ulster-Scots originated in the lowlands of Scotland, emigrated to Northern Ireland and then in the 1700s arrived in America. They landed in Delaware and Pennsylvania and migrated through North Carolina, Virginia, Kentucky and Tennessee.

The Scotch-Irish made important contributions to the new world. Bringing with them the skills of a cooper, a joiner, a wagon maker, a blacksmith, a hatter, a rope-maker, a weaver, and many other skills. Their education was very meagre, but in some fashion they acquired enough book learning to read the King James Version of the Bible, often their only book. They embraced the Presbyterian religion."

DORIS O. SINK, North Wabash Road, Marion, Indiana.

"The Scots-Irish held the valley between the Blue Ridge and the North Mountain and they formed a barrier which none could venture to leap."
- United States President Thomas Jefferson

"An overwhelming majority of the early settlers of Tennessee was Scotch-Irish. Every Tennessean descending from our first settlers is to be put down as of this people if he cannot prove his descent to be otherwise.
No church other than theirs, the Presbyterian Church, was founded in East Tennessee for 60 years after the first settlement."
- Kelly, Scotch-Irish Congress of Tennessee 1889

In addition to supplying their considerable soldiering prowess in the Revolutionary War effort, American citizens of Ulster stock provided the necessary finance in 1780 to help sustain the fight for freedom. Blair McClenaghan, from Co. Antrim, gave 50,000 dollars; John Murray, from Belfast, and three others from Scots-Irish families John Nixon, Thomas Barclay and John Nesbitt each donated 30,000 dollars; James Mease, from Strabane in Co. Tyrone gave 25,000 dollars while his uncle John, and John Dunlap, from the same town, both raised 20,000 dollars each and John Donelson weighed in with 10,000 dollars. Even by today's standards, the money contributed was huge.

★★★

27

Tennessee *records its appreciation*

A Proclamation approved by the Tennessee House of Representatives in May, 1995, acknowledges the outstanding contribution made by the Ulster-Scots in the history of the United States. It reads:

• "Whereas on June 24, 1314, Robert the Bruce, King of Scotland, defeated the English in the 'Battle of Bannockburn', which resulted in the sovereignty of Scotland being recognised and acknowledged by England; and

• Whereas, it was 'The Land Clearance" after the failure of 'The Rising of 1745' that brought thousands of people to leave Scotland; and

• Whereas, some Scottish immigrants came directly to this country; and

• Whereas, others left Scotland and came to Ireland before eventually coming to this country (i.e. Scots-Irish); and

• Whereas, any Scottish and Scots-Irish people settled in our State because areas such as our Tennessee mountains reminded them of their beloved highlands; and

• Whereas, they brought with them their love of independence, their religion, their crafts, their music and dances, their own colourful expressions, and their friendliness; and

• Whereas, many of the early leaders in Tennessee history were of Scottish or Scots-Irish descent, including three Presidents: Andrew Jackson, James K Polk and Andrew Johnson; John Sevier, our first Governor; General James Robertson, pioneer settler and founder of Nashville; Davy Crockett, member of the State Legislature, pioneer, hunter, member of Congress and hero of the Alamo; and Sam Houston, member of Congress, Governor of Tennessee and Governor of Texas; and

• Whereas, by 1885, one-half of Tennessee's Governors were of Scottish or Scots-Irish descent; and

• Whereas, important traces of Scottish and Scots-Irish culture remain with us today; traditions such as Southern hospitality, pride of religion, the Southern sense of honor and courtesy, country music and square dancing have their roots in Scotland and Ireland; and

• Whereas, it is appropriate that a day to set aside to specially recognise and commemorate the tremendous contributions made by people of Scottish and Scots-Irish heritage to the founding and development of Tennessee.

Now, I therefore I, Don Sundquist, Governor of Tennessee, pursuant to Public Charter 233 of the Public Acts of 1995 and in conjunction with Representative Howard Kerr and Senator Carl Koella, do hereby proclaim June 24 of each year as 'Scottish, Scots-Irish Heritage Day' and urge all Tennesseans to join in the observance of this day. Proclaimed in Nashville, this the 20th day of May, 1995."

The Proclamation is signed by Governor Don Sundquist, Representative Howard Kerr and Senator Carl Koella.

• Scots-Irish groups in Tennessee were behind the idea of the Proclamation and the leading protagonist for the concept was Tommy Rye, from Maryville in Blount Country outside Knoxville. Tommy is of Scots-Irish descent and his wife Betty is of direct Scottish ancestry.

28

200 years *of official US links with Belfast*

The United States of America has had a Consulate General in Belfast for 200 years and the office is one of the oldest American diplomatic posts in the world. The first-ever Consul General was James Holmes. He was appointed to the post on May 20, 1796 and arrived in Belfast in September of that year. Two hundred years on, the work of the office James Holmes opened has contributed to the strong relationship between Northern Ireland and the United States.

Kathleen Stephens, the present Consul General, took up her post in August, 1995, after diplomatic postings in Yugoslavia, Korea, China, Trinadad and Tobago. She confirms: "Wherever I have gone in Northern Ireland I have found strong ties of culture, commerce and friendship with the United States. Following on from President Clinton's visit to Northern Ireland last year, it is apt that we should have the opportunity to explore, celebrate and develop those links".

Some highly colourful personalities served as Belfast Consul, including General Lewis Richmond in 1880-81. Richmond was a distinguished Union Army officer in the American Civil War. He was engaged in the occupation of East Tennessee in 1863 and the capture of the Cumberland Gap from the Confederate forces.

Richmond was born in Rhode Island and in addition to holding the Belfast diplomatic portfolio, was later Consul General in Rome and United States Minister to Portugal.

Another was Dr. John Young, a native of North Antrim and a leading American attorney. Young was a friend of President Abraham Lincoln and ended up a diplomat in the Consular Service of the United States Government. The Youngs, originally lowland Scots, lived at Killagan near Ballymoney, but Dr. John Young's parents settled at Ballylough near Knockahollet. It was there that he was born in 1751.

He attended the Knockahollet school and a classical academy in Loughgiel; was trained for the Presbyterian ministry and educated at Old College, Belfast, now the Royal Belfast Academical Institution.

After completing his course at RBAI, he was put out on "trials" by the Presbytery of Route in North Antrim. The Presbytery, however, was shocked to hear Young's unorthodox views on a number of theological points, especially in relation to the Atonement and doctrine of Justification by Faith. He was branded an "Arian" and admonished by the Presbytery for his lack of orthodoxy and readiness to absorb strange ideas. Stubbornly, he refused to change and was prevented from entering the ministry of the Presbyterian Church in Ireland.

At the time he came under the influence of a newly-established group in Ireland, known as the Baptists. Their main centre was in Tobermore, Co. Londonderry, and John Young became a pastor of the Baptist Church and with his wife, formerly a Miss Orr from Ballymoney, conducted missions in various parts of Ulster. The number of adherents to the Baptist faith in Ireland were few and Young headed to America, where there were much better prospects for his pastorship. But in America, Young disagreed with the leaders of the Baptist movement and became a Unitarian. He studied law and, after graduating, became a barrister in Indianapolis, built up a big practice and emerged a notable personality in that state.

His politics in the United States was Republican and he campaigned in southern Indiana in support of President Abraham Lincoln. He was invited by Lincoln to join the diplomatic corps of the United States and was appointed American Consul to Belfast in 1861.

His office was in Donegall Square in the centre of the city and he lived in a cottage at the junction of Sandy Row and the Lisburn Road. During his five years as Consul in Belfast, Young regularly returned to his North Antrim homeland to renew his acquaintainship with relatives.

There have been 54 appointed Consuls or Consul Generals, with one Thomas W. Gilpin, serving two terms.

• James Holmes, Consul   (1796-1815)
• James Luke, Consul   (1815-20)

- Samuel Luke, Consul   (1820-30)
- Thomas W. Gilpin, Consul   (1830-42)
- James Shaw, Consul   (1842-45)
- Thomas W. Gilpin, Consul   (1845-47)
- Thomas H. Hyatt, Consul   (1848- never served in Belfast)
- James McDowell, Consul   (1848-49)
- H. Jones Brook, Consul   (1851 - never served)
- Cornelius McCauley, Consul   (1851 - never served)
- Valentine Holmes, Consul   (1851-53)
- John C. O'Neill, Consul   (1853-54)
- John Higgins, Consul   (1854-58)
- Theodore Frean, Consul   (1858-61)
- John Young, Consul   (1861-66)
- Gwynne H. Heap, Consul   (1866-67)
- Thomas K. King, Consul   (1867-69)
- James Rea, Consul   (1869-73)
- James M. Donnan, Consul   (1880-81)
- Lewis Richmond, Consul   (1880-81)
- Arthur B. Wood, Consul   (1881-84)
- George W. Savage, Consul   (1885-89)
- Samuel G. Ruby, Consul   (1889-93)
- James B. Taney, Consul   (1893-97)
- William W. Touvelle, Consul   (1893-1904)
- Samuel S. Knabenshue, Consul   (1905-09)
- Henry B. Miller, Consul   (1909-10)
- Hunter Sharp, Consul   (1911-20)
- William P. Kent, Consul   (1920-23)
- Henry P. Starrett, Consul General   (1923-26)
- Thomas D. Bowman, Consul General   (1927-31)
- Lucien Memminger, Consul General   (1931-37)
- Ernest L. Ives, Consul General   (1938-39)
- John Randolph, Consul   (1939-42)
- Parker W. Bukrman, Consul General   (1942-43)
- Quincy F. Roberts, Consul   (1943-48)
- William A. Smale, Consul   (1948-49)
- Wainright Abbot, Consul General   (1949-51)
- Ralph A. Boernstein, Consul General   (1951-53)
- Edward A. Anderson, Consul General   (1953-57)

- Nathaniel J. Lancaster Jr., Consul General   (1957-60)
- Cyril L. Thiel, Consul General   (1960-62)
- Eric M. Hughes, Consul General   (1962-65)
- Forrest K. Geerken, Consul General   (1965-66)
- Neil C. McManus, Consul General   (1967-71)
- Grover W. Penberthy, Consul General   (1971-74)
- Peter Spicer, Consul General   (1974-77)
- Charles R. Stout, Consul General   (1977-80)
- Michael A.G. Michaud, Consul General   (1980-83)
- Samuel Bartlett, Consul General   (1983-86)
- Robert P. Myers Jr, Consul General   (1986-89)
- Douglas B. Archard, Consul General   (1989-93)
- Valentino E. Martinez, Consul General   (1993-95)
- David Pazorski, (Acting) Consul General   (1995)
- Kathleen Stephens, Consul General   (1995-)

29

Counties *of Virginia*

The state of Virginia, founded as an American state on 25 June, 1788, has 95 counties

County	Main town
Accomack	Accomac
Albemarle	Charlottesville
Alleghany	Covington
Amelia	Amelia, C.H.
Amherst	Amherst
Appomattox	Appomattox
Arlington	Arlington
Augusta	Staunton
Bath	Warm Springs
Bedford	Bedford
Bland	Bland
Botetourt	Fincastle
Brunswick	Lawrenceville
Buchanan	Grundy
Buckingham	Buckingham
Campbell	Rustburg
Caroline	Bowling Green
Carroll	Hillsville
Charles City	Charles City
Charlotte	Charlotte Courthouse
Chesterfield	Chesterfield
Clarke	Berryville
Craig	New Castle
Culpeper	Culpeper
Cumberland	Cumberland
Dickenson	Clintwood
Dinwiddie	Dinwiddie
Essex	Tappahannock
Fairfax	Fairfax
Fauquier	Warrenton
Floyd	Floyd
Fluvanna	Palmyra
Franklin	Rocky Mount
Frederick	Winchester

Giles .... Pearisburg
Gloucester .... Gloucester
Goochland............... Goochland
Grayson.............. Independence
Greene.................. Stanardsville
Greensville.................. Emporia

Halifax .... Halifax
Hanover .... Hanover
Henrico .... Richmond
Henry .... Martinsville
Highland .... Monterey

Isle of Wight .... Isle of Wight

James City .... Williamsburg

King and Queen King and Quen
King George .... King George
King William ...... King William

Lancaster .... Lancaster
Lee ....Jonesville
Loudoun .... Leesburg
Louisa .... Louise
Lunenburg............... Lunenburg

Madison .... Madison
Mathews .... Mathews
Mecklenburg .... Boydton
Middlesex .... Saluda
Montgomery ..... Christiansburg

Nelson .... Lovingston
New Kent .... New Kent
Northampton .... Eastville
Northumberland ..... Heathsville

Nottoway .... Nottoway

Orange .... Orange
Page .... Luray
Patrick .... Stuart
Pittsylvania .... Chatham
Powhatan .... Powhatan
Prince Edward .... Farmville
Prince George .... Prince George
Prince William .... Manassas
Pulaski .... Pulaski

Rappahannock .... Washington
Richmond .... Warsaw
Roanoke ....Salem
Rockbridge .... Lexington
Rockingham .... Harrisonburg
Russell ....Lebanon

Scott .... Gate City
Shenandoah.............. Woodstock
Smyth .... Marion
Southampton .... Courtland
Spotsylvania .... Spotsylvania
Stafford .... Stafford
Surry .... Surry
Sussex .... Sussex

Tazewell .... Tazewell

Warren .... Front Royal
Washington .... Abingdon
Westmoreland .... Montross
Wise .... Wise
Wythe .... Wytheville

York .... Yorktown

30

The Scotch-Irish Society *of the United States of America*

The Scotch-Irish Society of the United States of America was founded in 1889 under the leadership of Colonel A.K. McClure and the Rev. John S. MacIntosh. Originally known as the Pennsylvania Scotch-Irish Society, its first constitution and by-laws set forth its purposes as:

"The preservation of Scotch-Irish history, the keeping alive the esprit de corps of the race, and the promotion of social intercourse and fraternal feeling among its members now and hereafter."

The Society has numbered among its members, leaders and builders in the nation's civic, business and professional life. The Scotch-Irish, blessed with energy, courage, enterprise, goodness of heart and devotion to duty, have left an indelible mark upon the communities where so many have zealously served, and upon the government in all its branches, where they have supported efforts to bring to reality for all the promise of a way of life the nation's founders envisioned.

The Society is first and foremost American. It believes that it can broaden, deepen and enlarge the principles from which the American nation has drawn the sustaining power for its development by recalling past achievements, remembrances and associations. The loyalty of the Scotch-Irish to the national ideals has been no better stated than by the first president of the Society, Dr. MacIntosh, when, in 1890, he said:

"Born and naturalised citizens, we give ourselves anew in this organisation to the land for which our fathers and friends gave their blood and lives. We are not a band of aliens, living here perforce and loving the other land across the sea. We belong to this land, and only recall the old that we may better serve the new, which is our own."

The Society, in 1949, organised the Scotch-Irish Foundation, a Pennsylvania non-profit corporation, to collect and preserve for public, educational and research use books, documents, family histories, letters, journals and historical material relating to the origin and history of the Scotch-Irish people in Scotland, Ireland and the United States. The Foundation is also empowered to receive gifts and legacies which are tax deductible. The Foundation's historical collection, which continues to be enlarged by purchase and donation of books, documents and genealogies, is maintained in modern, secure accommodations in The Balch Institute for Ethnic Studies, 18 South Seventh Street, Philadelphia, PA 19106.

The Foundation's archives contains a wealth of genealogical information. Those seeking information regarding their Scotch-Irish forebears are requested to employ a professional genealogist who may use the Foundation's library and archives to research the subject.

Membership in the Society is available to men and women who are of Scotch-Irish decent. The Scotch-Irish Society of the U.S.A. and the Scotch-Irish Foundation consider that the term "Scotch-Irish" generically designates those persons who are descended in either the male or female line from an ancestor or ancestors of Scottish origin, who emigrated to America from those parts of Ireland which were settled by people from Scotland about the year 1600 or thereafter. Membership is individually held. There is an application fee of $15.00. The annual dues are $20.00. Life membership is available by making a tax-deductible contribution of $300.00 to the Scotch-Irish Foundation.

Those who look to the future will wish to share in the prospering and strengthening of the Scotch-Irish Society as guardian of the history of the Scotch-Irish in America and as a Scotch-Irish presence in the support of the principles and ideals upon which the American nation was founded.

For information and membership applications, please write to:

The Scotch-Irish Society of the United States of America
and Scotch-Irish Foundation,
Box No. 181, Bryn Mawr, Pennsylvania 19010.

• The author of this book is an honorary member of the Scotch-Irish Society of the United States.

Distinguished American short story writer Edgar Allan Poe was the son of an Ulsterman David Poe, who emigrated to America in the early 19th century. Edgar Allan Poe created horror tales and was also the founder of the modern detective stories.

The poet Van Dyke pays his tribute to Francis Makemie, the founding father of Ulster Presbyterianism in America:

The Church

Oh, who can tell how much we owe to thee,
Makemie, and to labours such as thine,
For all that makes America the shrine
Of faith untrammelled and of conscience free?
Stand here, gray stone, and consecrate the sod
Where sleeps the brave Scots-Irish man of God.

Transatlantic *reviews*

"Billy Kennedy, through his book 'The Scots-Irish in the Hills of Tennessee', is a key figure in the revival of interests in Ulster-Scots emigration. The image of the rugged frontiersman pushing westwards over hard terrain is an attractive one for Ulster Protestants. But the political message from the history of the Ulster-Scots is not straight-forward. Support for the American revolution, says Kennedy, was not surprising. 'Our people were against the British'."
GARETH SMYTH, News Statesman, London.

"Belfast journalist Billy Kennedy has become somewhat of a folk hero between here and Nashville through his book 'The Scots-Irish in the Hills of Tennessee'. His quest to compile a 200-year history of the movement of the Scots-Irish Presbyterians to the American frontier brought him to Rogersville and many other historical communities in the Volunteer State."
ELLEN ADDISON, Editor, Rogersville Review, East Tennessee.

"A vivid and well-researched history of those early settlers, the frontiersmen and women who drove out west and left their imprint on what was to become the most democratic nation on earth".
BELFAST TELEGRAPH.

"Anecdote, record and historical detail not previously available in one volume, makes an intriguing reference took on, in the wider context of the United States, the Ulsterman and woman, abroad. A microcosm of the Scots-Irish diaspora".
ULSTER BELFAST NEWS LETTER.

"It is one of the great ironies of Irish history, the people who today are the most vocal in proclaiming their loyalty to the British Crown were probably the first republicans on the island of Ireland. It is a point well made by Billy Kennedy in his book 'The Scots-Irish in the Hills of Tennessee'."
DERRY JOURNAL.

"Northern Ireland journalist Billy Kennedy cannot see enough of East Tennessee and he appreciates the help and hospitality he has been shown during his trips to the region for research for his book. 'I have been made very welcome to the degree that you feel embarrassed', he said".
RICHARD MASON, Daily Times, Blount County, East Tennessee.

"Billy Kennedy's book is an excellent contribution to an often-neglected aspect of Irish history - the tale of the Irish Protestants who settled in vast numbers in the New World."

PORTADOWN TIMES.

"Asked why his book has been a hit in Ireland and America, Billy Kennedy replies: 'It's a true story. These people are real people. They existed and some are the most legendary in America'."

DAVID R. LOGSDON, Nashville Banner.

"Meticulously researched about those who played a key role in taming the American frontier. It is a book that is compulsive reading".

BALLYMENA GUARDIAN.

"An illuminating insight into the story of the trek from the fields of Ulster to the frontier of America. A book that is both a useful source of historical reference and a compelling story".

COLERAINE CHRONICLE.

"This richly informative book is a must for all lovers of history, whatever their nationality. Yes, it is that fascinating".

NEWRY REPORTER.

"When Billy Kennedy first arrived in Tennessee from his native Northern Ireland in 1993, his goal was to produce enough copy to fill up 16 pages of newsprint. He left Tennessee with enough material to fill up a book. So he did and the result 'The Scots-Irish in the Hills of Tennessee', a best-seller in both Ireland and America".

BRAD LIFFORD, Kingsport Times, East Tennessee.

"There is a resurgence of interest in Tenneessee's hill country that reminds the Irish of home. After all, many an Irishman came to East Tennessee when the United States was in its formative years. Along with the Scots, they fought for the nation's independence against Britain, the origin of their ancestors. Billy Kennedy, with his book 'The Scots-Irish in the Hills of Tennessee', is in the centre of this budding interest with East Tennessee".

FRED BROWN, Knoxville News-Sentinel.

Author's *acknowledgements*

- Walter K. Heyer, Executive Director - Museum of American Frontier Culture, Staunton, Virginia.
- Dr. John Rice Irwin, Director - Museum of Appalachia, Norris, Tennessee.
- Councillor Dr. Ian Adamson, Lord Mayor of Belfast.
- Tommy Rye, Maryville, Blount County, Tennessee.
- Don Troini (Artist) Southbury, Connecticut
- David Wright (Artist), Nashville.
- Trey Pennington, Emerald House Group, Greenville, South Carolina.
- Dr. Katharine Brown, Museum of American Frontier Culture, Staunton, Virginia.
- John Gilmour, Director - Ulster-American Folk Park, Omagh, Co. Tyrone.
- Dr. J. Roderick Moore, Director - Blue Ridge Institute and Museum, Ferrum College, Ferrum, Virginia.
- Alister McReynolds, Principal, Lisburn College.
- Captain R. Lynn McR Hawkins, Bluff City, Tennessee.
- Ronnie Hanna, Ulster Society, Banbridge, Co. Down.
- Fred Brown, Knoxville News-Sentinel, Tennessee.
- David R. Logsdon, The Nashville Banner, Tennessee.
- Councillor Rev. Eric Smyth, Past Lord Mayor of Belfast.
- Geoff Martin, Editor - Ulster News Letter, Belfast.
- Robert Anderson, Printer, Richhill, Co. Armagh.
- Kathleen Stephens, United States Consul, Belfast.
- Robin Greer, United States Consul, Belfast.
- Bobbie Sue B. Henry, Rockbridge County, Virginia.
- Louis Edmondson, BBC Northern Ireland.
- Patricia A. Hobbs, Director of Collections, Woodrow Wilson Birthplace and Museum, Staunton, Virginia.
- David Babelay, East Tennessee Historical Society, Knoxville.
- Judge and Mrs. George M. Cochran, Staunton, Virginia.
- Richard McMaster, Elizabethtown College, Pennsylvania.
- Jeanne Barkley, Knoxville.
- Dr. Susan A. Hanson, Museum of American Frontier Culture, Staunton, Virginia.
- Michael McDowell, Canadian Broadcasting Corporation, Washington.
- Albert and Maureen Mercker, Purcellville, Virginia.
- Barbara Parker, Department of Tourist Development, Nashville, Tennessee.
- Dr. Charles L. and Mrs. Sara Moffatt, Gallatin, Nashville.
- Elizabeth Queener, Nashville.

- Dr. Thomas W. Burton, Johnson City, Tennessee.
- Joe Costley, Belfast.
- Captain Carl Netherland-Brown, Rogersville, Tennessee.
- Brian Courtney, Portadown Times, Co. Armagh.
- Linda Patterson, Ambassador/Causeway Productions, Belfast.
- William Neill, Bangor, Co. Down.
- Professor Michael Montgomery, University of South Carolina.
- Robert H. Wallace, Knoxville.
- Lorene Lambert, Tennessee Department of Tourist Development, Nashville.
- East Tennessee Historical Society, Knoxville.
- Scotch-Irish Society of the United States of America.
- Lisa Cain Curran, Editorial Director, American Civil War Society.
- Chris McIvor, Librarian, Ulster-American Folk Park, Omagh.
- Christine Johnston, Ulster-American Folk Park, Omagh.
- Norman Hamilton, Ulster/Belfast News Letter.

PICTURES AND ILLUSTRATIONS

- David Wright (Artist), Nashville.
- Museum of American Frontier Culture, Staunton, Virginia.
- Woodrow Wilson Birthplace and Museum, Staunton, Virginia.
- Don Troiani (Artist), Southbury, Connecticut.
- Blue Ridge Institute and Museum, Ferrum College, Ferrum, Virginia.
- Bobbie Sue B. Henry, Rockbridge County, Virginia.
- Earl Palmer Collection, Blue Ridge Heritage Archive, Ferrum College, Ferrum, Virginia.
- Image of Sam Houston, Tennessee State Museum, Tennessee Historical Collection, Nashville.
- John Rush, Ulster News Letter, Belfast.
- David Babelay, Knoxville, Tennessee.
- Pacemaker Press, Belfast.
- Historical Atlas of Augusta County - Joseph A. Waddell/Jed Hotchkiss.

BIBLIOGRAPHY AND REFERENCES CONSULTED

- The Encylopaedia of the South - Robert O'Brien.
- Woodrow Wilson - Ronnie Hanna, Ulster Society.
- Woodrow Wilson - Life and Letters - Ray Stannard Baker.
- The Complete List of U.S. Presidents - William A. Degregorio.
- Woodrow Wilson - The Early Years - George C. Osborne.
- National Encyclopaedia of American Biography (Volume 4 Illustrated).
- President Woodrow Wilson's Irish and Scottish Heritage - Edward and Elizabeth Handy
- Who Was Who in the Civil War - John S. Bowman.

- The Scotch-Irish Letters in the Valley of Virginia - Bolivar Christian.
- The Lexington Presbyterian Heritage - Howard McKnight Wilson.
- Stonewall Jackson, Portrait of a Soldier - by John Bowers.
- Stonewall Jackson - Lieut. Col. G.F.R. Henderson, C.B.
- Ulster Emigration to Colonial America - R. J. Dickson.
- The Scotch-Irish - A Social History - James G. Leyburn.
- The Great Wagon Road - Parke Rouse Jun.
- Folks from Larne - George West Diehl.
- The Peopling of Virginia - Bean R. Bennett.
- Stories of the Great West - Theodore Roosevelt.
- Ulster Sails West - W. F. Marshall.
- The Family of John Lewis, Pioneer - Irwin Frazier.
- Samuel Doak (1749-1830) - William Gunn Calhoun.
- Samuel Doak - Earle W. Crawford.
- Patriots at Kings Mountain - Bobby Gilmer Moss.
- Belfast News Letter, 250 Years (1737-1987).
- One Heroic Hour at Kings Mountain - Pat Alderman.
- Houston and Crockett, Heroes of Tennessee and Texas - An Anthology.
- The Overmountain Men - Pat Alderman.
- Land of the Free; Ulster and the American Revolution - Ronnie Hanna.
- With Fire and Sword - Wilma Dykeman.
- America's First Western Frontier, East Tennessee - Brenda G. Calloway.
- The Tinkling Spring (Headwater of Freedom).
- The Mathews Family in America - I.C. Van Deventer.
- Woodrow Wilson - August Heckscher.
- History of Augusta County.
- The Ulster-American Folk Park, How It All Began - Eric Montgomery.
- The Leath/Leeth/Leith Family History.
- Thomas Jefferson and His World - American Heritage.
- Timber Ridge Presbyterian Church (The Old Stone Church).
- Two South Rivers of the Shenandoah and James Rivers - Bobbie Sue B. Henry.
- Six Months of an American Adventure - Lamar Alexander.
- Lexington - Religion and Marriage.
- Frontier Preacher (the Rev. Samuel Black) - Natalie K. Black.
- Old Farm Tools and Machinery, An Illustrated History - Percy C. Blandford.
- God's Frontiersmen, The Scots-Irish Epic - Rory Fitzpatrick.
- Annals of a Scotch-Irish Family - William H. Whitsitt.
- The Scotch-Irish of Augusta.
- A. Wallace Heritage - Norene Wallace Bony.
- The Scotch-Irish and Ulster - Eric Montgomery.
- Staunton, Virginia, A Pictorial History - David J. Brown.
- The Highest Call - Ronnie Hanna, Ulster Society.

Thanks

I would gratefully acknowledge the tremendous help and assistance given to me in compiling this book by so many people in the United States.

From across the Appalachian region and from other American states I have received a shoal of information on the Scots-Irish families who settled on the frontier 200/250 years ago. I fully appreciate the time and effort taken by those to whom the Scots-Irish tradition and culture means so much and I greatly value the many letters of support sent to me for this project. I hope that through this book, and my previous work 'The Scots-Irish in the Hills of Tennessee', many people will come to know and understand the sacrifices made by a strong resolute people in creating a civilisation and a structured way of life in a wilderness. The United States would not be the nation it is today had it not been for the pioneering spirit of the Scots-Irish. Their valour and outstanding achievements make them a very special people.

Billy Kennedy

The author can be contacted at:

49 Knockview Drive,
Tandragee,
Craigavon,
Northern Ireland,
BT62 2BH.

Remember

There is a future and a need to achieve;
likewise a history, whose passing we grieve.
Beyond this, a birthright - a cultural truth -
a memory that echoes from earliest youth -
and calls me more strongly with each passing season.

In a fiddle, a banjo, my ancestors speak -
they awaken inside me when bagpipes creak.
My grandfathers call from across generations
and beckon my soul to the dark Appalachians;
they call me with longings and deep intuitions,
disdaining my world and its foolish ambitions.

They call me in reveries and wistful daydreams;
they call in the thunder of whitewater streams.
They call from clear pools beneath tumbling fountains;
they call from the forests of haunted black mountains.
From deep-shadowed coves that no sunlight has kissed,
and from boulder-strewn summits enshrouded in mist.

Remember our passing the length of your days -
forget not our language, remember our ways.
Cleave to these valleys and cherish these hills,
and nurture the spirit that progress kills.
Those things that most matter are not done for gain;
lose who you are and all else is in vain.

These dark Smoky Mountains remember your name -
remember when first the Logue family came -
when Scots-Irish fiddles first shattered the still,
as lonesome and high as these Tennessee hills.
Those wild Celtic spirits from over the sea
still wander these woods with the dark Cherokee.

Though the dark cloud of industry covers the land,
remember this holy earth where you now stand.
Someday you'll return to your true mountain home
from the cities and highways you restlessly roam.
No peace will you find as you tarry there yet;
what the mind can't remember, the blood can't forget.
What the mountains have given, the blood can't forget.

- Robert Ashley Logue,
Tennessee.

Index

V

Van Dyke 194

W

Waddell Rev James 142
Wagoner Captain Andrew 145
Wallace — Peter (147-9), Elizabeth (148-9), Michael (148), James (148), Andrew (148), William (148), Michael (148), Hannah (148), Hugh Campbell (148), Samuel (148-9), Samuel Jun. (148), Andrew 11 (148), David (148), General Lew (148), Susannah (148), Peter Jun. (148), William Alexander Anderson (149-150)
Ware Captain Samuel 66
Washington —Augustine (70), George (36, 41, 69-71, 86, 117, 134, 140-1, 176), Lawrence (71), Mary (70)
Wayland John W. 37
Whitefield Rev George 150, 155

Whipple William 39
White — Edward H. (36), Hon. Hugh L. (163), James (60, 144), Moses (144)
Whitsitt — William (150), Rev James (150), Elizabeth (150)
William 111 (King) 91
Wilson —Woodrow (41, 45-52, 100, 106, 157), James (47-8), Anne Adams (48), Dr Joseph Ruggles (45, 48, 52), Rev Thomas (47), Ellen Louise Axson (50), Edith Bolling Galt (50), William (150), Barbara McKane (150), Sarah Alexander (150), William Jun. (150), Esther (150), Margaret (150)
Wood — Michael (148), Arthur B. (187), William (148)
Woodrow — Rev Thomas (47), Jessie (48)

Y

Young Dr John 185-87